S0-BIL-667

ETHNIC PRIDE

Explorations into Your Ethnic Heritage
Cultural Information--Activities--Student Research

WITHDRAWN

By Greta Barclay Lipson, Ed.D.
Jane A. Romatowski, Ed.D.
The University of Michigan-Dearborn

Illustrations by Sheri Simons

Cover design by Susan Kropa

Copyright © Good Apple, Inc., 1983
ISBN No. 0-86653-121-1
Printing No. 98765432

GOOD APPLE, INC.
BOX 299
CARTHAGE, IL 62321-0299

The purchase of this book entitles the buyer to reproduce student activity pages for classroom use only. Any other use requires written permission from Good Apple, Inc.

All rights reserved.Printed in the United States of America at Whitehall Company, Wheeling, IL.

INDIANA STATE UNIVERSITY LIBRARY

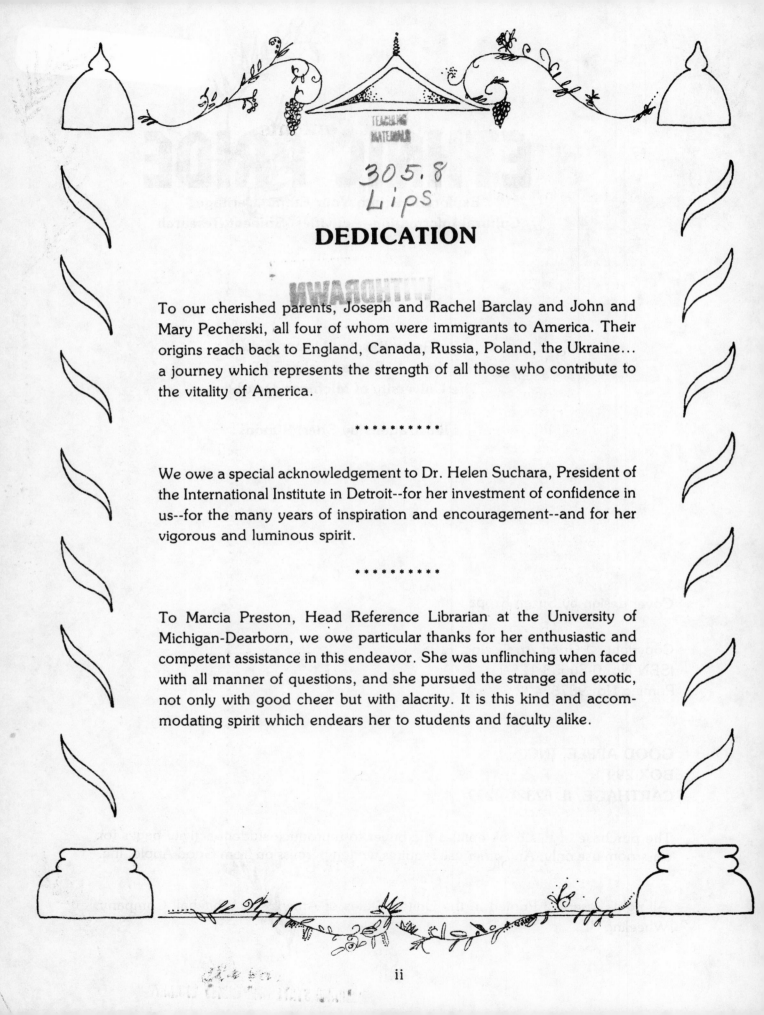

305.8
Lips

DEDICATION

To our cherished parents, Joseph and Rachel Barclay and John and Mary Pecherski, all four of whom were immigrants to America. Their origins reach back to England, Canada, Russia, Poland, the Ukraine... a journey which represents the strength of all those who contribute to the vitality of America.

* * * * * * * * * *

We owe a special acknowledgement to Dr. Helen Suchara, President of the International Institute in Detroit--for her investment of confidence in us--for the many years of inspiration and encouragement--and for her vigorous and luminous spirit.

* * * * * * * * * *

To Marcia Preston, Head Reference Librarian at the University of Michigan-Dearborn, we owe particular thanks for her enthusiastic and competent assistance in this endeavor. She was unflinching when faced with all manner of questions, and she pursued the strange and exotic, not only with good cheer but with alacrity. It is this kind and accommodating spirit which endears her to students and faculty alike.

Table of Contents

Ethnic Groups in the United States 1
Introduction 3
How to Use This Book 5
Letter to Parents 7
Ethnic Form for Parents 8
Chapter 1 - NAMES 9
    For the Teacher 10
    Student Activities 12
    Personal Research 15
Chapter 2 - CHRONOLOGY 16
    For the Teacher 17
    Student Activities 18
    Personal Research 22
Chapter 3 - IMMIGRATION 23
    For the Teacher 24
    Student Activities 27
    Personal Research 31
Chapter 4 - GEOGRAPHY 32
    For the Teacher 33
    Student Activities 35
    Personal Research 39
Chapter 5 - RITUALS 40
    For the Teacher 41
    Student Activities 42
    Personal Research 45
Chapter 6 - CALENDARS 46
    For the Teacher 47
    Student Activities 49
    Personal Research 53
Chapter 7 - HOLIDAYS 54
    For the Teacher 55
    Student Activities 57
    Personal Research 60
Chapter 8 - ETHNIC FOODS 61
    For the Teacher 62
    Student Activities 63
    Personal Research 67
Chapter 9 - FOLK MEDICINE AND SUPERSTITION 68
    For the Teacher 69
    Student Activities 71
    Personal Research 75

161435

Chapter 10 - MEMORIES, NOSTALGIA, ARTIFACTS 76
    For the Teacher 77
    Student Activities 85
    Personal Research 90
Chapter 11 - FINE ARTS - FOLK ARTS 91
    For the Teacher 92
    Student Activities 94
    Personal Research 99
Chapter 12 - LANGUAGE 100
    For the Teacher 101
    Student Activities 102
    Personal Research 108
Chapter 13 - FAMOUS PEOPLE 109
    For the Teacher 110
    Student Activities 112
    Personal Research 120
Chapter 14 - GAMES AND TOYS 121
    For the Teacher 122
    Student Activities 124
    Personal Research 129
Chapter 15 - HISTORICAL PLACES AND NATURAL WONDERS 130
    For the Teacher 131
    Student Activities 133
    Personal Research 138
Chapter 16 - FASHION AND ADORNMENT 139
    For the Teacher 140
    Student Activities 143
    Personal Research 148

ETHNIC GROUPS IN THE
UNITED STATES

The word "ethnic" derives from the Greek word "ethos" meaning nation, people. An ethnic group is made up of people who share the same national origin, who may be of the same race and religion. They share a particular culture, language, history, and background. One may add or subtract from the list, but it must always include a common and distinctive tradition shared by the group. Racial similarity does not, of itself, describe an ethnic group. The following list of ethnic groups in the United States is drawn from the HARVARD ENCYCLOPEDIA OF AMERICAN ETHNIC GROUPS (Cambridge, Mass.: Harvard University Press, 1980; Stephan Thernstrom, Editor).

Ethnic Groups in the United States

Acadians
Afghans
Africans
Afro-Americans
Albanians
Aleuts
Alsatians
American Indians
Amish
Appalachians
Arabs
Armenians
Asians
Assyrians
Australians and
 New Zealanders
Austrians
Azerbaijanis
Bangladeshi
Basques
Belgians
Belorussians
Bosnian Muslims
Bulgarians
Burmese
Cambodians
Canadians
Cape Verdeans
Carpatho-Rusyns
Central and South
 Americans
Chinese
Copts
Cornish
Cossacks

Creoles
Croats
Cubans
Czechs
Danes
Dominicans
Dutch
East Indians
English
Eskimos
Estonians
Filipinos
Finns
French
French Canadians
Frisians
Georgians
Germans
Greeks
Gypsies
Haitians
Hawaiians
Hungarians
Hutterites
Icelanders
Indochinese
Indonesians
Iranians
Irish
Italians
Japanese
Jews
Kalmyks
Koreans

Kurds
Latvians
Lithuanians
Luxembourgers
Macedonians
Maltese
Manx
Mexicans
Norwegians
Pacific Islanders
Pakistanis
Poles
Portuguese
Puerto Ricans
Romanians
Russians
Scots
Serbs
Slovaks
Slovenes
South Africans
Spaniards
Swedes
Swiss
Tatars
Thai
Turkestanis
Turks
Ukrainians
Vietnamese
Welsh
Wends
West Indians
Zoroastrians

"The melting pot (concept) said that as you come to America, you forget who you are, you speak English, you act white, Anglo-Saxon, Protestant middle-class just like everyone else. But the WASP middle-class has never been in the majority in this country. They are only about 14% of the population. Everybody in America is an ethnic."*

Jim Anderson, Director of the U-M Ethnic Heritage Research Studies Program
The University of Michigan
Ann Arbor, Michigan

Introduction

We, in America, are either native Americans or overwhelmingly a nation of immigrants from other lands. The notion of the "melting pot" has been eclipsed by the new wave of pride and curiosity about our different beginnings. A more appropriate descriptor for America is to call it a "pluralistic society." In acknowledgement of this, there is a need for developing pride in ethnic heritage. From this new awareness, one is better able to reach out toward others and appreciate the unique contributions to the quality of life which come from all of us. The diversity of custom, geography, language, and the arts to be explored in each ethnic group yields a rich human tapestry. The intention of this book is to help teachers and students find their own colorful ethnic strands. This highly personalized book will help take a comprehensive look at heritage and origins. Beyond the usual superficial approach, ETHNIC PRIDE will explore family history, the arts, music, language, famous people and places, as well as the usual "folksy" customs which tend to be the most popularized.

---

*From the *Detroit Free Press*, Sat., May 15, 1982. Written by staff writer, Ruth Seymour.

The appreciation of others begins with an appreciation of self. Pride in one's heritage can mark the beginning of a developing sensitivity to others. In America's classrooms, we find a living example of the multicultural fabric of this country. Accepting and prizing this multicultural bounty can truly be a liberating experience. It can free us from the tyranny of prejudice and bigotry and can safeguard cultural freedom for us all.

ETHNIC PRIDE is an attempt to move students and their teachers beyond trite and stereotypic information about ethnic groups. At times, such stereotypic information has reinforced inaccuracies and has designated groups depriving them of their right to cherish and take joy from their heritage. The goal of this book is to assist teachers in protecting and nurturing each person's self-image, self-concept, sense of self. This can be done by starting with an exploration of ancestral backgrounds. Those students who are unable to trace their heritage to a specific ethnic group should be given the option of studying the group of a choice.

ETHNIC PRIDE is a book for today's classroom. One need only consider that, in the decade of the seventies, over three million people emigrated to the United States of America. One need only look at a sample midwestern, metropolitan school system to see that in the late 1970's over 6,000 school children were identified as nonnative speakers of English representing over seventy different languages and as many cultures. One need only consider that these school figures would triple or quadruple in certain metropolitan areas in the Southwest, Southeast or Northeast. Tapping the rich resource should not be difficult.

How to Use This Book

No teacher can be expected to be familiar with all the varied cultural backgrounds represented by the students in any one classroom. This book contains guidelines and activities which will help both teacher and student direct their study and research. The information gathered will derive from two sources: the country of origin and/or ethnic information from regional areas in America such as Appalachia. The choice of sources should be made on the basis of what is most meaningful for the student and what is appropriate for the lesson.

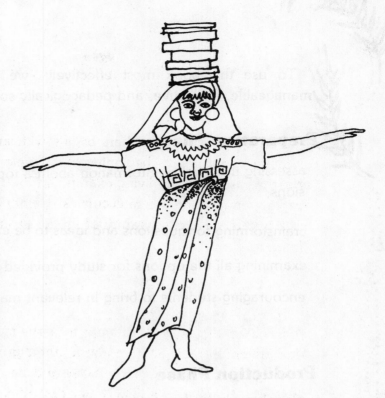

ETHNIC PRIDE focuses on concepts related to ethnicity and develops those concepts cross-culturally, illustrating ties among all cultures. In this way, the book differs significantly from social studies texts in that it has a double focus: to elicit pride in one's own ancestry and simultaneously to appreciate the ancestry of others.

The book is organized according to conceptual areas of study. Each conceptual area of study provides:

> information for the teacher
> suggested classroom activities
> personal research pages for the student

In selecting the classroom activities, the teacher should assess the competencies of the students and select activities which are most suitable. With modification, activities can be made more simple or more sophisticated. The teacher's own judgment and creativity will be a strong factor.

The sections designated as "For the Teacher" are not intended as giveaways for the students. It should not take the place of the student's own research and discovery. Rather, it is intended to define the area of study and suggest some possibilities for the content of the assignment.

To use this book most effectively, we suggest a teaching model that is manageable, facilitative, and pedagogically sound. It consists of three phases:

Preparation Phase

assessing the level of information about a topic through initial whole-class discussions,

brainstorming for questions and ideas to be explored through study and research,

examining all the options for study provided under suggested activities, and

encouraging students to bring in relevant material on the topic.

Production Phase

planning whole-class activities which deal with selected topics,

preparing outlines, interview questions, and identifying people to interview,

arranging for library time as necessary,

arranging for ethnic places to visit,

arranging for ethnic resource people to visit,

planning for writing time, creative preparation of materials and rehearsal time.

Presentation Phase

scheduling specific times when the entire class can discuss what has been learned,

arranging for specific days and times when individual students can present their findings or display their products, and

planning for time to appreciate and discuss individual and group creative efforts.

Letter to Parents*

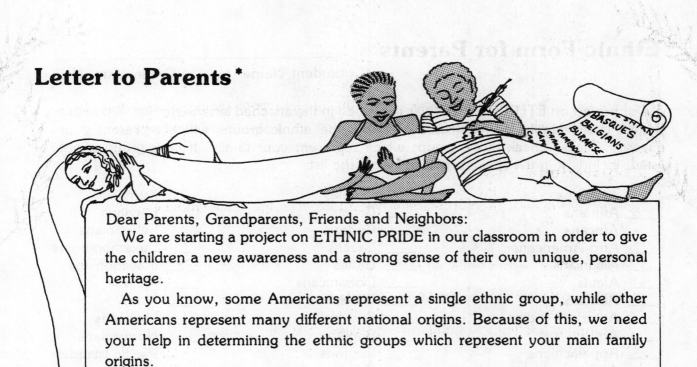

Dear Parents, Grandparents, Friends and Neighbors:

We are starting a project on ETHNIC PRIDE in our classroom in order to give the children a new awareness and a strong sense of their own unique, personal heritage.

As you know, some Americans represent a single ethnic group, while other Americans represent many different national origins. Because of this, we need your help in determining the ethnic groups which represent your main family origins.

On the attached sheet you will find a list of ethnic groups in the U.S.A. This list is drawn from the Harvard Encyclopedia of Ethnic Groups in the U.S. Please check the group or groups which indicate your ancestral roots. If your ethnic group (or the group you wish your child to study) is not listed, please write in the name of that group on the blank lines provided on the form.

It is our objective to help the students collect and research information which has personal value for each of them. In addition, we are including opportunities for the children to interview friends and relatives who may have interesting stories and memories on many of the topics covered.

From this study we expect that children will develop projects that will express their heritage. Beyond this is the more important objective of nurturing respect for the contribution of each cultural group to America's richness.

The plan is to reach out and share the results of this classroom enterprise with other teachers and students in the school, with parents, and with all interested members in the community. We look forward eagerly to your valuable cooperation and participation.

Sincerely,

_____

Classroom Teacher

*Suggested by TEACHING STRATEGIES FOR ETHNIC STUDIES, by James A. Banks, Allyn & Bacon, Inc., 1979.

Ethnic Form for Parents

Student Name   Grade   Rm. No.

Our project on ETHNIC PRIDE was explained in the attached letter. Our first step in this project is to identify, for purposes of study, the ethnic groups which represent your ancestry. Please check those groups which represent your family. If your group is not listed, include it in the space provided below the list.

____ Acadians	____ Creoles	____ Kurds
____ Afghans	____ Croats	____ Latvians
____ Africans	____ Cubans	____ Lithuanians
____ Afro-Americans	____ Czechs	____ Luxembourgers
____ Albanians	____ Danes	____ Macedonians
____ Aleuts	____ Dominicans	____ Maltese
____ Alsatians	____ Dutch	____ Manx
____ American Indians	____ East Indians	____ Mexicans
____ Amish	____ English	____ Norwegians
____ Appalachians	____ Eskimos	____ Pacific Islanders
____ Arabs	____ Estonians	____ Pakistanis
____ Armenians	____ Filipinos	____ Poles
____ Asians	____ Finns	____ Portuguese
____ Assyrians	____ French	____ Puerto Ricans
____ Australians and	____ French Canadians	____ Romanians
New Zealanders	____ Frisians	____ Russians
____ Austrians	____ Georgians	____ Scots
____ Azerbaijanis	____ Germans	____ Serbs
____ Bangladeshi	____ Greeks	____ Slovaks
____ Basques	____ Gypsies	____ Slovenes
____ Belgians	____ Haitians	____ South Africans
____ Belorussians	____ Hawaiians	____ Spaniards
____ Bosnian Muslims	____ Hungarians	____ Swedes
____ Bulgarians	____ Hutterites	____ Swiss
____ Burmese	____ Icelanders	____ Tatars
____ Cambodians	____ Indochinese	____ Thai
____ Canadians	____ Indonesians	____ Turkestanis
____ Cape Verdeans	____ Iranians	____ Turks
____ Carpatho-Rusyns	____ Irish	____ Ukrainians
____ Central and South	____ Italians	____ Vietnamese
Americans	____ Japanese	____ Welsh
____ Chinese	____ Jews	____ Wends
____ Copts	____ Kalmyks	____ West Indians
____ Cornish	____ Koreans	____ Zoroastrians
____ Cossacks		

List additional groups here: _____

Please return this list by: _____
                                                          Date

Your kind cooperation will help us get our project started.

Chapter 1

NAMES

Saroj Ghoting

Me Llamo Arnoldo Francisco Ricardo de La Fuente de Reyes

" Your name is like a golden bell hung in my heart."

Beagle

9

Names

Names give an impression, set a tone or make a statement to the people who hear them. A young man named Parks Rinehart may prefer to be called by his nickname Sparky, while Lizzy West may wish desperately that her friends use her given name, Elizabeth. Either way, the identity of names is strong and lasts a lifetime.

A first name is also known as a given name. We all feel keenly about our names since they are attached to us from infancy on. There are often variations of our formal names used by people close to us who address us informally. But whatever the variations might be, our names give us a sense of ourselves, and we are rarely neutral in our reaction to them.

In Europe and England in the twelfth century the use of *surnames* or family names came into fashion. This happened because as the population of a village or settlement grew, it became more difficult to sort out the proper identity of all the Johns and Marys and Davids and so the system of giving last names was devised as a way out of the confusion. And this was where the fun started. Family names were derived from a variety of sources. Some were based upon the following possibilities:

A FATHER'S NAME (A patronym) In England if your father's name was Ben, your name became son of Ben or Benson. In Italy if your father's name was Marco you became De Marco. In Scotland the son of Donald was McDonald. Informally, in Arabic, you might be Ibn Saud or son of Saud.

AN OCCUPATION If you were the man who made flour, your name might be Miller. In Germany one who made solid gold rings was called Goldfinger. In Bulgaria a Kovac was a smith who fashioned objects out of iron, and a Frobrisher in England was a person who furbished or polished armor. In France, Saine described a man who butchered and sold pork.

10

PHYSICAL CHARACTERISTICS In Switzerland if you had white hair or a light complexion you might be called Wyss (white). In Germany a small person could be named Klein (small). In Czechoslovakia one with a big head might be known as Kotrba, and in England one with great strength would be named Armstrong.

A PLACE Some people took the name of a city or the place in which they lived. Berg in German means mountain. Ono in Japanese means small field. Dembinski in Polish signifies a dweller in or near an oak wood. Del Rio in Spanish identifies a person who lives near the river.

In England, by the end of the 14th century, surnames of fathers had become hereditary and were passed down through families for generations. Historically and in modern times, last names are often changed to more closely resemble the language or local name patterns of an adopted country for ease of spelling and pronunciation. Still, many people prefer to retain their original family names.

Parallelling European history, we find that Native Americans did not, initially, use surnames either. Popular Indian names, such as Osceola, Powhatan, and Squanto, were prevalent but were not family names. We came to know the Indians by English translations of their names, such as Black Hawk, Kicking Bird, and Spotted Tail. Before the arrival of the Europeans, the Indians did not have a need for family names. Much later, when the government placed agents to work on the reservations, there were further changes of Indian names for purposes of identification. There was often no apparent influence of the genuine Indian names on subsequent family names.

A different pattern for the acquisition of family names is evident among the Black slaves who, after the Civil War, adopted surnames of their choice. Before the Emancipation, only the northern Blacks had surnames. There is some evidence that certain names were preferred and have survived to the present. Some American Blacks, in modern times, have chosen to emphasize their ethnicity by adopting names more reflective of their African heritage. Some of these name changes have been: Le Roi Jones, the playwright, now known as Amiri Baraka and Cassius Clay, now known as Muhammad Ali.

Student Activities

1. Write out your complete given name, middle name, surname, and nickname if you have one. Be prepared to share and discuss with your classmates any information you find about the meanings of your names. Contribute your name card to a class bulletin board display or collage of names.

2. Ellis Island is in New York Harbor and was a station for the entry of immigrants into the U.S. from 1894 to 1954. It was sometimes called "The Gateway to the New World." Recently the newspaper had an account of a change of name which happened to an immigrant on Ellis Island in 1914, and was a rather frequent occurrence at that time. A Greek immigrant whose name was Alexander was unable to spell it for the immigration officials. Finally, he gave them a name he was able to spell which was Bakalis, because it meant "grocer" in Greek and he had been a grocer in his homeland. Does anyone in your family know of a similar name change which occurred in the family due to problems with the English language or other difficulties due to understanding?

3. What customs are followed in your ethnic group when a child is given a name? Explain the custom of naming a child after a father, relative or friend. What other sources (Bibles and holy books) are used for names?

4. The surnames Smith, Brown and Jones are the most common names in the United States. Since Smith is a name based upon an occupation it appears in many languages. Smith in French is Ferrier, in Spanish Herrero, in Hungarian Kovacs, in Polish Kowalczyk, in German Schmidt, in Dutch Smit and in Italian Ferraro. Find the most common names in your ethnic group and list them.

5. If you had the opportunity to give yourself the name of your choice, which would express your ethnic heritage, what would the name be? Explain.

6. Find out how to write your name in the language of your ancestors. How does your name sound in that language?

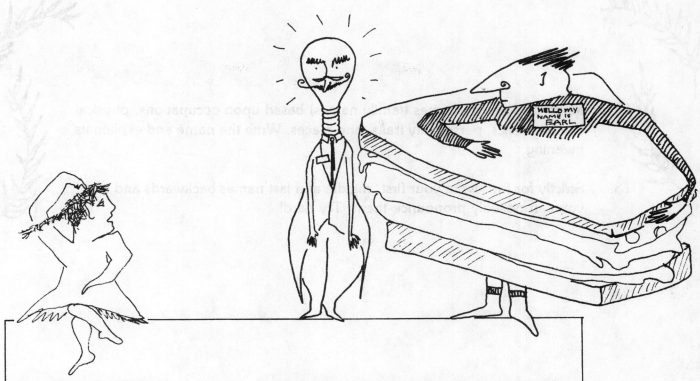

7. What are the different names in your language or family which express love and affection? For example, the American Indian name Uggams is derived from a phrase meaning "sweet one."

8. In the custom of your people, what happens to your mother's family name (maiden name) after marriage? Some children use their mother's maiden name as a middle name. Some women prefer to retain their maiden names after marriage. Explain old and new practices among your family members.

9. In Chinese, Chan means old, Gee means well-mannered, and Jin means metal or gold. Look in a book of given first names to find out what your name means. Make a list of the first, middle and last names of your closest relatives. Include nicknames which they have had in their lives. Find the meanings of those names. Do you have any favorites among those meanings? Identify your favorite meanings with a red star.

10. Look in the telephone directory. Find one family name for each letter of the alphabet. Try to have your list represent as many different ethnic groups as possible. Consult others in your class to determine ethnic names.

11. The sandwich was named after the Earl of Sandwich. The name for the electrical unit of power, a watt, comes from the Scottish inventor James Watt. The cardigan sweater was named after the 7th Earl of Cardigan. What other words, names of products, etc., were named after people?

12. Make up some surnames (family names) based upon occupations, physical characteristics, personality traits, and places. Write the name and explain its meaning.

13. Strictly for fun, write your first, middle and last names backwards and see if you can possibly pronounce them. Try hard!

NAME _____

DATE _____

PURPOSE: To understand the source and meaning of my name and the names of others and to trace any changes in family names.
To appreciate the cultural heritage of all names.

1. On the back, list the persons you interviewed. Also list books, magazines, pamphlets, family documents and any other sources used for information.

2. THE MOST EXCITING THINGS I LEARNED:

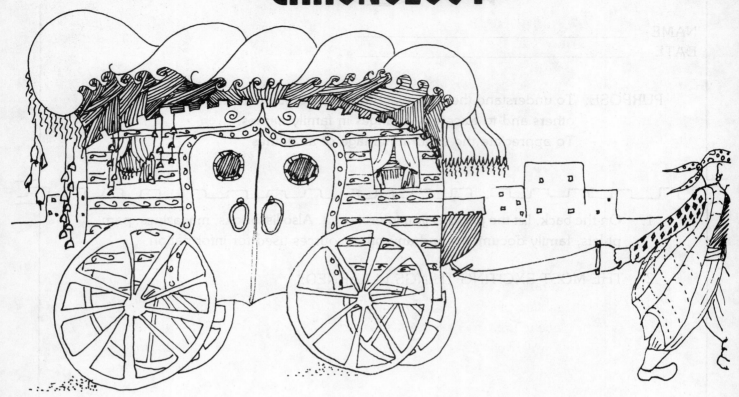

Chapter 2

"Time, you old gypsy man,
will you not stay,
Put up your caravan
Just for one day?"

Ralph Hodgson

Chronology

Chronology means the science of measuring time in fixed segments and of dating events and interesting periods and arranging them in the order of occurrence. Each of us has our place in time and each of us through our work, profession, or interests makes a mark. All our great scientific, technological, academic and cultural achievements are built upon the work of others who come before us. It is this awareness that can help us feel a part of some great design rather than as isolated lights which flicker and die. We become aware of our own "self" as a special link in an ongoing chain. There is comfort in that. Have you had the experience of looking at old photographs or browsing through memorabilia and saying, "That happened after Grandpa married Grandma" or "I did that in the fourth grade" or "This picture was taken before your aunt came to the United States." These references were historical. They had a place in time. When we examine photographs, documents, and memorabilia in this way, we often experience a feeling of fullness as human beings knowing that we are a part of something greater than our own individual moment in time and space.

It is common to refer to humans in the great constellation of history as being small and insignificant, like a grain of sand. But we do know that all people collectively make changes in the world. Ultimately, the combined energy of each of us effects change in the social fabric. We offer up our contribution to fulfill our own needs and ambitions and also for the greater good of all those during our lifetime and all of those who will follow. One single person *can* make a difference. One single person *does* make a difference and human history bears this out.

We can help our students experience these feelings and arrive at a sharper sense of self and a clearer view of how that "self" looks historically through the activities suggested in this area of exploration.

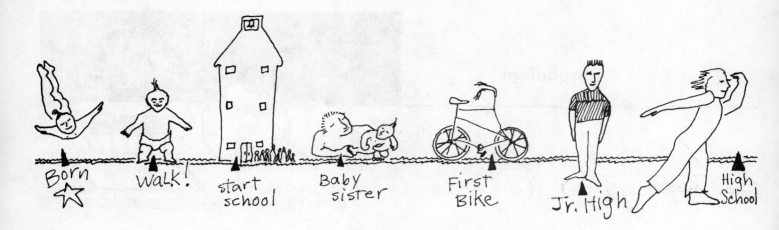

Born ☆   Walk!   start school   Baby sister   First Bike   Jr. High   High School

Student Activities

1. Make a personal time line. Start with your birthday. Collect as much information about yourself as you can. Write each important event starting with your birth date and place on a 3 x 5 card. Place the date in the upper right-hand corner. Arrange all your cards in the order of occurrence. Now get some mural paper. Draw a thick line through the middle for your time line. Lay your cards out to allow for good spacing, illustrations, or the gluing on of photographs or documents. Place a large red dot for each event. Rewrite what you have on your 3 x 5 card or paste the card in that spot. Illustrate each event or decorate with pictures or other mementos. In the center and at the top of your time-line mural, write your name in bold letters.

2. Make your family time line. Concentrate on your family unit for a family history. On 3 x 5 cards, list major events in your immediate family's history including births, graduations, exciting trips, awards won, special anniversaries, deaths, etc. Use the same directions given for your personal time line. When you have completed arranging your information, title your mural appropriately "The History of the Kocyn Family" or "The Majian Family History" or something similar.

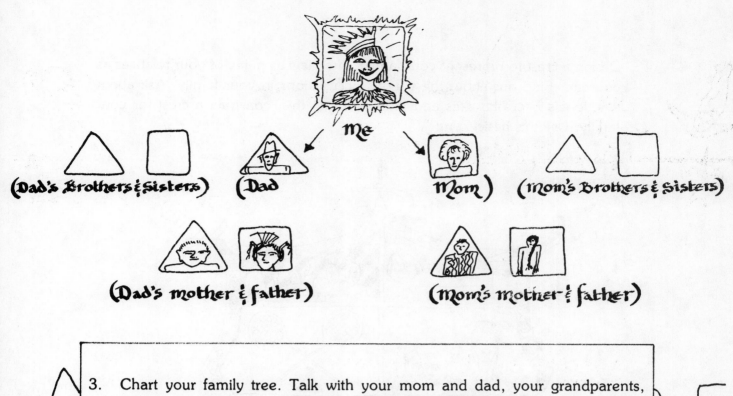

(Dad's Brothers & Sisters) (Dad   Mom) (Mom's Brothers & Sisters)

(Dad's mother & father)   (Mom's mother & father)

3. Chart your family tree. Talk with your mom and dad, your grandparents, aunts, uncles, cousins. Try to collect as much information from each member as you can to help construct your family tree. Remember to ask about the maiden names of all the married women in your family history. On a large poster board, diagram your family line. Write each male member's name on a triangle and each female member's name on a square. Start with yourself at the top of the poster board and begin placing other members of your family below. Use one line for each generation. Go as far back as you can. If you have small photographs and the space to paste them in, do so.

4. Design a crest to represent your family. Interview as many of your relatives as you can. Find out about the various occupations in your family. Ask about everyone's interests, likes and dislikes. From this, construct a crest for your family. Use this basic form:

Here are some suggestions about what you might want to place in each square:

your family's nicest trait or quality
an animal or bird to represent your family
a flower to represent your family
a color to represent your family
a religious symbol for your family
a hobby or a sport which characterizes your family
a popular food in your family
an important object in your family

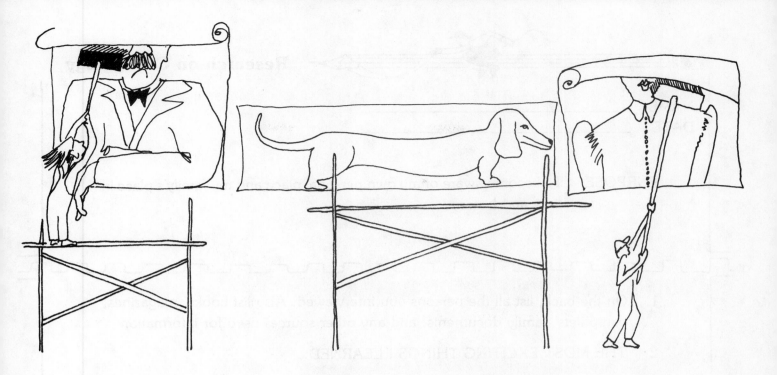

5. Construct a dated family scrapbook. Talk to your parents and relatives and collect a number of photographs from various times in your family's past up to the present. If possible, duplicate important documents--an old birth certificate, an award, a special letter, special invitations, birth announcements, etc. Arrange these in chronological order. Paste them on separate pages using only rubber cement for the best effect and the least damage to the paper. For each item, write a descriptive statement of two or three sentences. After proofreading and editing, enter your statement below the picture or document. Use your imagination in describing a photo, for example, "Smell those burgers at the old family cookout!" Create a sturdy cover for your book so that your photographs are well protected.

6. Create a book which honors a special person in your family. Think about someone in your family of whom you are very proud. Write an article or an essay giving as much information about that person as you can. Write in such a way that you make the life and character of that person come alive. At the end of your essay, share with the reader all the qualities this person has that make you so proud. If you have a picture of this special family member, it may be included with your essay and mounted inside a construction paper folder to be used as a very special gift.

NAME _____

DATE _____

PURPOSE: To become aware of my own personal place and my family's place in time and history.

1.   On the back, list all the persons you interviewed. Also list books, magazines, pamphlets, family documents, and any other sources used for information.

2.   THE MOST EXCITING THINGS I LEARNED:

Chapter 3

IMMIGRATION

" Give me your tired, your poor,

Your huddled masses yearning to breathe free,

The wretched refuse of your teeming shore.

Send these, the homeless, tempest-tost to me,

I lift my lamp beside the golden door! "

Emma Lazarus

From the poem: "The New Colossus" inscribed on a tablet in the pedestal of The Statue of Liberty, in 1903.

Immigration

FOR THE TEACHER

To depart from a land is called emigration. To enter a new land is immigration. Since the first English settlers came to this country in 1607 to escape prejudice and tyranny, America has been held dear in the hearts of many who left their homelands. "America," they said, "is the golden land, the land of opportunity." And some even said, "The streets are paved with gold!"

Immigrants came to this country hoping to find a better world. Many suffered great hardship and deprivation to make the long voyage across the sea. There was the pain of leaving loved ones, friends and everything that was familiar. Some were sure they would never see their families again! It took great courage and most often desperation to chance a new life in a land where the language, people, customs and values were strange. And it is still true today that such dislocation creates social, economic, and psychological problems for newcomers.

> "...but some immigrants have found the doors to America less open than others and the path ahead strewn with more obstacles. Until recently, the great American ideal of justice and equality for all did not seem to apply to those who differed radically in race or cultural background from our so-called founding fathers. . . . Though we fall short of our vaunted ideals, we are moving steadily toward their achievement."*

Within the past four centuries the one thing that all Americans have in common is that we are all descended from immigrants, or we *are immigrants*. The one group that is an exception to this is the American Indian. But still, before history was written, thousands of years ago, the forebears of the Indians came to the Western Hemisphere by walking across a land bridge believed to have been in existence 20,000 years ago.

---

*NISEI by Bill Hosokawa, Wm. Morrow and Co., N.Y., 1969.

Because many immigrants came willingly to this country, it gave them the strength and spirit to endure the horrible conditions of the long voyage to America. But one group, for whom immigration was not voluntary, were the Black Africans who were brought to America in chains in the 1600's and 1700's as slaves. The death and disease of the Blacks far exceeded the horror of any other people who came to these shores. Those who survived are the ancestors of slaves who spent centuries in servitude.

Another group of especially exploited newcomers were the Chinese. The gold rush in California in 1848 ushered in the arrival of 41,000 Chinese men to the main port of entry in San Francisco. Instead of riches from "Jinshan," the mountain of gold, they suffered discrimination and the severe deprivation of any human rights. After the gold fever, the need for cheap hard "coolie" labor on the Transcontinental railroad systems was a factor which attracted these underpaid immigrants. At peak employment, out of 10,000 railroad workers, 9,000 were Chinese who had come to "Mei Kwok" or "the beautiful land" for a new life.

Later, in 1869, other Asians with a different culture arrived when their government permitted its citizens to leave. These were the Japanese. The first Japanese laborers arrived in Honolulu in 1869. They were not, in truth, the first immigrants, for they were hired as contract laborers to work on the plantations. They intended to return to Japan. The first true colonizers on the U.S. mainland founded the Wakamatsu Colony. These were the Japanese who settled in Sacramento, California, to establish their colony and farm 600 acres of land. They brought 50,000 three-year-old mulberry trees to start a silk farm, tea seeds, and other varieties of native plants and seeds. The colony did not flourish and in two years dispersed. The Japanese who arrived later came in very small numbers (2,230 entered the U.S. in 1891) and they responded to the need, once again, for cheap labor in America.

Within the confines of our own country, we find significant migration from one area to another. One of the major movements for families in this country has been from Appalachia to a variety of northern or midwestern urban centers. Appalachia is the name given to an economically deprived region in the Appalachian Mountains of the eastern U.S. It includes parts of thirteen states, ranging from southern New York to eastern Mississippi. About 18 million persons live in Appalachia. Family incomes and the literacy rate there are much lower than the national average. This area includes among others, the Blue Ridge Mountains, the Great Smoky Mountains, the Allegheny Mountains, and the Cumberland Mountains. The movement of these people to other points in the United States represents an atypical pattern of emigration inasmuch as it occurs within the borders of the United States.

Presently, in the decade of the 80's, we find that Blacks are the first largest minority. The second largest minority in the United States is Americans of Hispanic or Latin origin. Among these are Mexican, Cuban, Puerto Rican, Spanish and Portuguese people. The first large group of Mexican Americans, about 80,000, was acquired through the annexation of Texas by the U.S. and by our victory in the U.S.-Mexican War. Between 1845 and 1854 the U.S. came to own half the territory which formerly belonged to the Republic of Mexico. There was a slow growth of the Mexican-American population for a time until the great influx of immigration started in 1890 when cattle was replaced by cotton in Texas and there was a great need for laborers. Throughout these transitions many Mexicans lost their land through unscrupulous American manipulation and new laws which they did not understand. Of the thousands of peasants who streamed across the border there were those who came out of desperate poverty and those who hoped to escape the bloodshed of the Mexican Revolution in 1910. There is a spirit and a sense of common destiny shared by Spanish-speaking people which is embodied in the ethnic term "La Raza" meaning "The Race." It has become a rallying force for social identity and social change.

In the common destiny of immigrants, there had to be someone brave enough and stout-hearted enough to make the journey away from their native land. Someone in every family, recently or long ago, arrived in this country as an immigrant. They came by boat or plane, by bus, car, train, or on foot. They arrived at a seaport, at an airport, or at a land border. For some it is easy to trace their heritage to a land outside the borders of the United States. Others will only be able to trace their heritage to regions within the borders of the United States. But for all, the journey into the past will provide information for today to be cherished now and for many tomorrows.

Student Activities

1. The people in your family who came to this country as immigrants arrived at a port of entry or crossed a land border. Some of these entry points may be: Ellis Island in New York; San Francisco, California; Seattle, Washington; San Diego, California; Chula Vista, California; or Detroit, Michigan. Where did members of your family originally enter this country? Be prepared to contribute to a class list.

2. Try to find out the reasons your ancestors had for emigrating. Why did they choose the city in which they settled? Write a paragraph explaining this information.

3. In an encyclopedia find "Immigration and Naturalization Service." Describe the duties of a person who enforces immigration laws for this United States government agency.

4. Try to figure out the dates and numbers of people in your family going back about four or five generations to your great-grandparents and your great-great-grandparents. Make a chart of as many generations as you can in your family. Start with yourself and your own birthplace.

Your Name _____ Born 1970

Name of Mother _____ Born 1945

Name of Father _____ Born 1940

Names of Grandparents: Grandma born circa   1920

                                Grandpa born circa   1915

Names of Great-Grandparents, etc.

You may estimate the age difference as 25 years between parents and their children if you do not know the actual birth dates. Use the word "circa" when you use such estimates. The word "circa" is an interesting word that has a convenient use. It means an approximate date--circa 1925 "about 1925."

GRANDMA BESSIE DATER
CIRCA 1900

UNCLE YOUSIF ZAKARIA
CIRCA 1899

5. If your parents came over from the old country and you were born in the U.S., that makes you a first-generation American. If your grandparents came over and your parents were born here, that makes you a second-generation American. A generation is usually considered to be the number of years between the birth of parents and their children. The time between generations is different in all families. The Japanese Americans have simplified this and have a different way of accounting for each of their generations in America as follows:

ISSEI	First generation who came to America (born in Japan)
NISEI	Second generation (born in America)
SANSEI	Third generation (born in America)
YONSEI	Fourth generation (born in America)

6. When immigrants come to a new land they are very anxious to be able to work and earn a living. Some were lucky because they had skills that would help them find a job in America. Others had to take whatever employment they could find. What jobs or occupations did your relatives have before they came to the U.S.? What jobs were they trained to work at as young people? What do they do now? If there is a difference between the jobs then and now, can you explain the reasons for this?

7. Make a list of your closest family members. Next to their names write their places of birth. Make a world map and put a red dot at the site of each birthplace.

8. Pretend that you are emigrating to America. Pick a date for your emigration. How old are you at the time of your emigration? Pretend you are keeping a diary. When you arrive in America record your first three days. Include your feelings and impressions, remembering that your age will make a big difference. Share your diary with your classmates.

9. If you could emigrate to any city in the world today, which one would it be? What do you find attractive about the location you chose? What other information would you consider necessary to know before making the move? Why?

10. Everybody needs a welcome! The Wampanoag Indians were the first to welcome the Pilgrims to Plymouth in March 1621. They were greeted by Samoset, the Indian who had learned a cordial phrase from English fishermen who visited the coast of Maine. He said, in a most gracious manner, "Welcome, Englishmen." Who welcomed your ancestors to this country or region? What arrangements were made for them? Who were the significant people who helped them? Were there organizations or institutions which helped them?

11. If your family has moved a great deal in this country from region to region, draw a map of the U.S. and draw color coded lines showing this movement. Include the approximate date of each point of settlement and names of family members living there. One of the major movements for families in this country has been from Appalachia to a variety of northern or midwestern urban centers. Your map will give you a clear picture of how members of your family have located themselves across the United States.

NAME _____

DATE _____

PURPOSE: To learn about other countries or regions in America from which my ancestors came.

1. On the back, list the persons you interviewed. Also list books, magazines, pamphlets, family documents and any other sources of information.

2. THE MOST EXCITING THINGS I LEARNED:

Chapter 4

GEOGRAPHY

"The country of every man is that one where he lives best."

Aristophenes

Geography

FOR THE TEACHER

Geography, the study of the earth's features, includes also the study of the changes or contributions to earth by humans and their activity. It is not surprising to find that the word "geography" derives from Greek words meaning "description of the earth." The Greeks, we discovered, were among the first of Western peoples to systematically study and record geographic information and to relate one piece of geographic information to another. In prehistoric times, knowledge of geography was limited to the area of the earth that could be reasonably traversed by foot. Today, to be a truly informed world citizen, a much broader knowledge of geography is essential. The distribution of land, water, population, minerals, plant life, animal life, and the effects of climate on various regions of this planet helps people make those decisions which lead to physical and economic survival. The ability of human beings to act upon the geographic characteristics of their environment and to sustain themselves over time is witness to their power of adaptation. Out of such adaptations have come advances in agriculture, new food items, products, technology and ideas which have left their mark on civilization.

It is possible for us to describe ourselves according to height, weight, age, sex or the size of our jeans, shoes, shirts, socks and gloves and even head size for hats. Countries, too, are described in terms which give important clues to their style of existence. Such data tells us how the character of a country is affected and influenced by the reality of its vital statistics. Is it a country rich in natural resources? Is the farming meager and difficult? Is the country on the sea and pulsing with rich commerce and trade? Is the country rich and powerful in terms of population and location? Is the temperature warm and balmy or are the winters cruel, long and unremitting? Is the country small, isolated and vulnerable? How rich, how poor? Countries, like people, are alive and dynamic with very real personalities of their own.

There appears to be a natural curiosity and awareness about geography in most people. Deciding where to live, what to wear, the style of dress, what to plant and grow, where to vacation, with whom to trade are all responses to geographic information of one kind or another. The place of our birth is a matter over which we have no control. But in our maturity, if we have a choice about where we are to live, it is often based upon the geographic conditions which we prefer. If we love the sun, our move may be to find it in a southern clime, in all its glory. If we are cold weather fans, we will look to the more frigid climes to please our passion for the ice and snow.

nepal

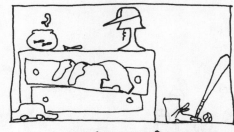
state of Disarray

china

Student Activities

1. Using available maps and globes, find the country of your ancestors. Examine it carefully and record the following information:

    What is the latitude and longitude of the country?
    Which countries border it?
    Which bodies of water are closest to it?
    Which bodies of water or waterways are within its borders?
    How much area does it cover?
    Which continent is it in?
    Is it larger or smaller than the state in which you live?
    Does it have mountain ranges, deserts, or other unusual geographic characteristics?
    What is its capital?
    What are its major cities?
    What is its mean temperature?

2. Using encyclopedias, almanacs, literature you received from travel agencies or embassies, record the following information:
    How many people live in the country?
    What is the official language spoken?
    Can you find a sample of the written language if it is different from American English?
    What does the country's name look like when written in its own language?
    What educational opportunities are there for the citizens?
    Which religions are important?
    Which national holidays are celebrated?
    Is there a popular national sport?
    Where do most people live?
    How do they govern themselves?
    What do they use for money?
    Are there some popular foods in the country?
    What does the nation's flag look like and what does it symbolize?

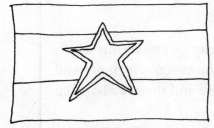
yugoslavia

whoositz

ceylon

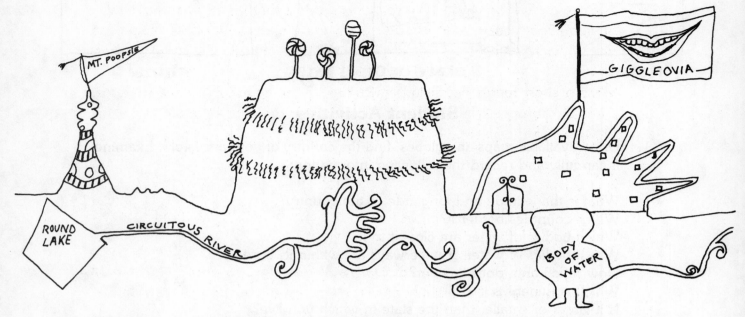

3. Using newspapers, current magazines, ethnic publications, postcards, travel brochures, *etc.*, make a scrapbook collection to represent the country of your ancestors. Look for newspaper articles which have datelines from your ancestral country. A dateline is not a date. It is the beginning line of the story stating *where* the event took place. You may also find American articles which describe an event in your ancestral country. Look for pictures and maps in newspapers and magazines. Remember to look at the world weather charts for temperature readings. The business section, too, contains international information which you could incorporate in your scrapbook.

4. Using a variety of maps and the globe, prepare a map report on your country which would include a series of three maps:

The Country Alone:
   - A map of the country only. Make it large enough so that you can draw in mountain ranges, deserts, rivers, and bodies of water. Locate with large dots the major cities and the capital. Put the national flag in one corner.

The Country and Its Continent:
   - A map of the continent in which your country resides. Label all the other countries and the significant bodies of water.

The Cities of My Ancestors:
   -A map of your country circling the name of the city or cities from which your ancestors came. Draw a line from the city to the side of the paper and write down the names of those who were born there and their relationship to you.

5. Prepare a travel brochure which would provide a tourist with interesting information about your ancestral country. Include a map, a list of scenic spots to visit, and interesting facts about the country. Draw or paste in colorful pictures.

6. Write a short report describing agriculture in the country you are studying. Describe farm practices, the kind of food grown, the animals raised and some popular dishes served.

7. Each area in the world has made its own contributions to the world. The monks brought the silkworm to Italy; the Bing cherry was cultivated in Oregon by a Chinese immigrant named Bing in 1875. (Cherries were grown 4000 years before that in China.) The seeds for cantaloupes (a variety of muskmelon) were originally imported from Armenia. The first cabbage grown in America came from a cabbage patch planted by Dutch colonists on Long Island. Make a list and describe several contributions of your ancestral country to the world.

8. Did you ever wonder who was brave enough to eat the first tomato, which was considered poisonous? Or who in the world would want to eat a thistle-like plant called the Jerusalem artichoke? Select an exotic fruit or vegetable with which you have had no experience. In one paragraph describe the fruit or vegetable, where it is grown and write an imaginary account of how you think it was discovered to be edible. In the second paragraph, finish the job by recording the results of your research and telling the "real story."

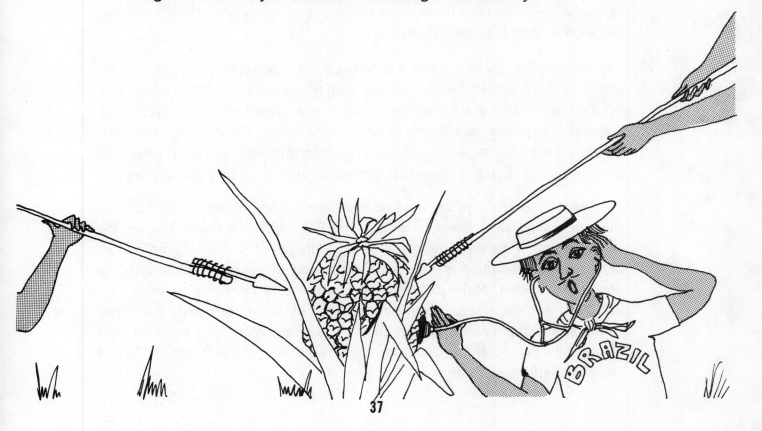

9. If possible, write a letter to a person, a newspaper, a school, a tourist bureau or any other organization in the country of your ancestors. Tell them about your Ethnic Pride project. Ask them for any free material which would add to your information. Be sure to save the stamps!

10. There are many different ways to study geography. The following are some of the areas into which geography can be divided and studied:

> world geography
> human geography
> mathematical geography
> biological geography
> political geography

Consult reference books and find all the different ways in which geography can be studied. Pick at least three areas which sound interesting, describe them, and explain why they are important.

11. Climate and the seasons make a difference in the life-style of people. If you visited Italy you would find that the big meal is eaten at noon. Most businesses will then close down and people go home to have a noon rest. Later in the day, business is resumed and dinner is eaten very late in the evening. How are customs, eating habits, sleep schedules, recreation, sports and work schedules affected by the climate or seasonal temperatures in your heritage country?

12. If it were not for the zoo, we would never have the opportunity to see some of the interesting beasts, birds, serpents, and fish which are found all over the world. Some of the creatures are especially intriguing! A good example of an animal which is fascinating is the marsupial found in Australia, which carries its young in a pouch. Marsupials may be as small as a mouse or as large as a kangaroo (which is seen on Australia's coat of arms). Research the many creatures which are native to your ancestral country. Which one captures your imagination the most? Explain to the class as part of a project entitled "Weird and Wonderful Creatures!"

NAME _____

DATE _____

PURPOSE: To understand how the geography of my ancestral homeland contributes to its character and the life-style of its people.

1. On the back, list the persons you interviewed. Also list books, magazines, pamphlets, family documents and any other sources used for information.

2. THE MOST EXCITING THING I LEARNED:

Chapter 5

RITUALS

"ceremony is really protection, too,
in times of emotional involvement...
If we have a social formula to guide us
and do not have to extemporize,
we feel better able to handle life."

Amy Vanderbilt

Rituals

A ritual is a set form or system of rites practiced by people in observance of special events which happen in life. These practices may or may not be religious, but all humans, universally, acknowledge the cycle of life in which we are all participants. These are the times of birth, baptism, birthdays, confirmation, coming of age, marriage, anniversaries, graduations, and finally death and mourning. The term "rites of passage," is a comprehensive term signaling the completion of one state of life and the passage into another. Some examples are: baptism into a religious fold, achieving adulthood, and entering marriage. These are occasions which we share with family and friends. Whether joyous or sad, we take time out from our daily lives to honor people and happenings. All rituals express the particular tradition and culture of an ethnic group. An example of this is the Bar Mitzvah (for a Jewish boy) or Bas Mitzvah (for a Jewish girl). It is on this 13th birthday one is considered to be a responsible person who has passed into adulthood. For this occasion the birthday celebrant studies an assigned portion of the Torah (the first 5 books of the Old Testament written in Hebrew). The portion assigned to the reader of the book is called the muftar. It must be studied for many months and fully understood so that the girl or boy can translate it into English and appreciate the ancient wisdom and tradition which it carries. The young candidate stands at the great book on the Sabbath--Friday night or Saturday morning--as did the ancestral fathers, and faces a congregation in a temple or a synagogue, while reading or chanting the prayer. One must follow the words in the Torah with a special pointer since the book is too holy to touch with one's fingers. The experience requires great effort and concentration for the initiate who wants earnestly to perform without making a single mistake. The party which follows is for both adults and children who share in the festivities and gift-giving in honor of this religious observance.

41

Tibet

Switzerland

WEDDING HEADDRESSES

Sikkim

Student Activities

1. Discuss the meaning of life's rituals with the adults at home. Bring in a list of the special observances in your ethnic group having to do with birth, baptism, coming of age, marriage, anniversaries and finally with death. Contribute this information to a large class list. Explain the rituals as they are listed. Which ones have you never heard of before? Which ones would you like to learn more about? Select one of interest to you and write a page describing the event.

2. Bridal veils were worn by Roman women 2000 years ago. In the American tradition, a bride at a formal ceremony will wear a white gown with a bridal veil (to protect the bride from evil spirits). What is the costume of the bride, the groom and special guests in your family's tradition? What ethnic touches can you identify?

3. The ancient custom of wearing wedding rings is thought to have its beginning as a symbol of eternal and cyclical life. It is put on the ring finger of the left hand because the vein in that finger was assumed to run straight to the heart. What jewelry or other items are exchanged or worn by the wedding celebrants in your culture?

4. When an American baby is born, fathers may pass out cigars, lollipops, pens, etc., to friends, relatives and co-workers to announce their joy. Belgians, traditionally, offer dragees which are almonds coated with a layer of soft sugar. How is the birth of a baby acknowledged or announced in your ethnic group?

5. Norwegians do not slice wedding cake, for it is against tradition. The cake is baked in rings and made with almond paste, icing and bonbons. The married couple simply break off chunks to serve to their guests. Is there a special kind of wedding cake and custom in your family tradition?

6. A Korean child's first birthday is observed by dressing the little one in traditional costume. The youngster is seated and surrounded with cookies, fruit, rice cakes and offered objects which symbolize a career in the future. The idea is that the first thing the baby takes will indicate the future vocation. Are there special ways in which birthdays are celebrated in your family? "Sto Lat" is a Polish song sung at birthdays. It is a wish for 100 more years of happiness. Can you find out about an ethnic song or greeting in your family, especially used at birthdays?

7. Among Christians, Jews and Muslims, burial in the ground is typically practiced. Among Buddhist and Hindu peoples, cremation is typically practiced. Many of these practices have to do with the religious belief regarding the passage of the body from this world to another. Among the Jews, the funeral ceremony takes place the very next day following the death. The body is not embalmed or prepared to lie in state. This is because Hebrew Scriptures say that after death one must return to the elements as soon as possible. Among Christians, and others, the body lies in state for 1-3 days during which time it may be viewed by family and friends. Funeral customs vary greatly from one culture to another. There are, however, common practices shared by all people. Friends and relatives are informed of the death; the body is prepared for a final resting place; a ceremony or service is conducted; the body is buried, cremated, or placed somewhere; and there is a period of mourning. What are the practices of your cultural group when a death occurs?

8. Ask your parents, grandparents and older relatives to describe their weddings complete with all the details. Where did it take place, who officiated and what was served? Were there musicians, and what did they play? How were gifts given? Was the marriage arranged by parents or a matchmaker? Explain.

9. Make a list of all the life events for which you have a family gathering (do not include holidays). Select one which, for you, was the most exciting and describe it. Perhaps you were the central character. In some cultures, the birth of the first son is occasion for a special celebration. If this is true in your tradition, describe the events and the reasons for them.

10. Christian baptism is the sacrament of admitting a child into Christianity or a particular Christian church by sprinkling water on the child or by immersion. This is symbolic of purifying the spirit and washing away sin. The Methodists have a religious ceremony which is called "dedication," for the newly born. Explain a birth ceremony as practiced in your family, religious or ethnic group.

11. Hispanic communities celebrate a girl's 15th birthday with a very fancy party known as a "quincerano." This is a recognition of a girl's entry into young womanhood. The church ceremony and the party introduces her into society and is a time of dressing up in beautiful gowns for the young woman and her friends. Are there special events or parties in your family's tradition when young people are introduced to society? Describe the events and the ages at which these events occur.

NAME _____

DATE _____

PURPOSE: To understand the meaning of rituals and the need for all human beings to observe life events in a special way.

1. On the back, list the persons you interviewed. Also list books, magazines, pamphlets, family documents and other sources used for information.

2. THE MOST EXCITING THINGS I LEARNED:

Chapter 6

CALENDARS

"Monday's child is fair of face,

Tuesday's child is full of grace,

Wednesday's child is full of woe,

Thursday's child has far to go,

Friday's child is loving and giving,

Saturday's child has to work
        for its living,

But a child born
        on the Sabbath Day

Is fair and wise and good
        and gay."

—Rhyme

Calendars

FOR THE TEACHER

Primitive peoples depended upon hunting and fishing and the harvest of fruits and berries to sustain them. They noticed, of course, that their search for food and its abundance was determined by changes throughout the year. All of these changes fell into a definite pattern as did daylight and darkness, or the phases of the sun, moon and the stars. Both terrestrial and celestial events had a recurrent rhythm, and people watched for these clues so that they would be ready to plant and harvest during the warm spells and be prepared for bad weather when food was scarce.

The Egyptians were among the first to use a predominantly solar calendar, meaning that their days were measured by the position of the sun in the sky. The earliest *recorded* date we know about is found in the Egyptian calendar and corresponds to the year 4236 B.C. in our present day calendar system. The calendar underwent many changes throughout the years. It was important to arrange the system of measuring time so that the calendar was an accurate predictor of the seasons as they occurred throughout the year. The calendar we now use and which is most widely used throughout the world is the Gregorian calendar designed by Pope Gregory XIII in 1582 A.D.

Our use of B.C. and A.D. is critical to understanding the major division of time in the modern calendar. When the letters B.C. follow a date, it means the date is historically placed in the time "Before Christ." By contrast, when the letters A.D. follow a date, it means after the birth of Christ--in Latin, "Anno Domini," or "In the Year of the Lord." People who are non-Christians may choose to use the designation B.C.E., which means "Before Christian Era." This is an interesting variation, though we do not see it used often.

There are other calendars which are still observed in modern times. The Jewish people in their religious observance use the Hebrew calendar which is thought to have had its beginnings in the year 3761 B.C. This calendar is supposed to measure time from the earth's creation. Hebraic dates have after them the designation A.M.

This stands for the Latin "Anno Mundi" or "in the year of creation." The Hebrew calendar is based on lunar (moon) cycles and is not exact, having twelve months, six with 29 days and six months with 30 days. Sometimes the Jewish year has 354 days or may have 383 days. Seven times during every nineteen-year period an extra 29-day month called Veadar is added. This takes place roughly between our months of March and April at which time the Hebrew month Adar (which approximates March) is given 30 days rather than 29.

The Islamic calendar is used by religious Muslims and is based upon Prophet Muhammed's life. The first year of the calendar takes as its date the time when the Prophet fled from Mecca and Medina. The Saudi Arabian government holds the Islamic calendar as its official calendar. Following Islmaic dates, are the letters A.H. which means "in the time of the emigration" or the year of the Prophet's move expressed in Latin as "Anno Hegirae." This calendar has twelve months, alternately 30 and 29 days long.

The Chinese calendar, which is based on the moon, was supposed to have been invented by Emperor Huang-Ti, in 2637 B.C. The Chinese calendar is based on a twelve-year cycle. Each year in this cycle is represented by an animal whose characteristics are to be attributed to the birthday person as well as to the year itself. Included in the student activities is a chart which places the animal signs by the date of birth. The chart is illustrated in twelve year segments. The Chinese New Year may fall as early as January 20 but no later than February 20.

Having explored the rich history of the calendar, it is clear that we owe a debt to the past--since the systemizing of time has contributed greatly to the orderly conduct of human affairs.

Student Activities

1. The days of the week and the numbering of years were dealt with in interesting ways in various cultures. Below you will find the way in which the Saxons named the days in the week in the 5th and 6th Centuries A.D. You will also find a list of cultural groups and the current dates according to those calendars. Select a group you would like to know more about, research that group's approach to the calendar and be prepared to explain it to your classmates.

SAXON

DAYS OF THE WEEK
Sun's Day
Moon's Day
Tiw's Day
Woden's Day
Thor's Day
Frigg's Day
Saterne's Day

OTHER CULTURAL CALENDARS

For our date, 1983, the calendars of other cultures will list this year as follows:

BYZANTINE	7492
CHINESE	4681
GRECIAN	2295
HEBRAIC	5744
JAPANESE	2643
MOHAMMEDAN	1404
ROMAN	2736

2. In many cultural groups, specific days are set aside for worship and rest. Sometimes these days are called Sabbath days. When is the Sabbath observed by your people? What are the Sabbath days of other people? (Sunday-Christian, Friday-Mohammedans, Saturday-Jews.) Look up the word Sabbath in the dictionary and explain what the term means.

3. Write a paragraph describing what would happen in your life if, all of a sudden, all of the calendars in the world were destroyed. What would happen at school, at work, at home, or on a farm?

4. If you were to fill out a calendar with dates which were especially important to you, what would these be? Design a twelve-month calendar scrapbook using one sheet for each month. Make squares for each day large enough to allow for entries. Write in the events throughout the year which have special meaning for you and your family.

5. Find your birth date on this Chinese zodiac calendar chart. Find the animal sign which represents your year of birth.

YEAR OF BIRTH	ANIMAL
1969 - 1981 - 1993	Rooster
1970 - 1982 - 1994	Dog
1971 - 1983 - 1995	Pig
1972 - 1984 - 1996	Rat
1973 - 1985 - 1997	Ox
1974 - 1986 - 1998	Tiger
1975 - 1987 - 1999	Rabbit
1976 - 1988 - 2000	Dragon
1977 - 1989 - 2001	Snake
1978 - 1990 - 2002	Horse
1979 - 1991 - 2003	Goat
1980 - 1992 - 2004	Monkey

Find the year in which you were born to determine your own animal sign. List all the names in your family, birth dates and their corresponding animal signs.

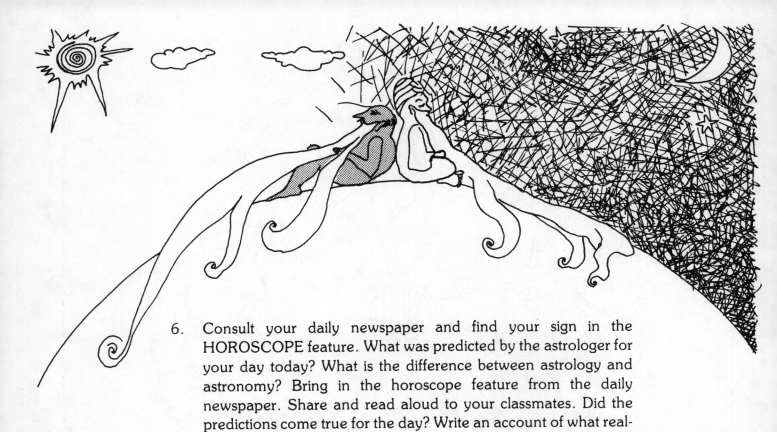

6. Consult your daily newspaper and find your sign in the HOROSCOPE feature. What was predicted by the astrologer for your day today? What is the difference between astrology and astronomy? Bring in the horoscope feature from the daily newspaper. Share and read aloud to your classmates. Did the predictions come true for the day? Write an account of what really happened.

7. A consideration of the measurement of days, weeks, months and years would not be complete without the study of time. Humans began to observe the recurrence of natural events-- night and day, the rising and setting of the sun, the phases of the moon, and the ebb and flow of the tides. And as these events were recorded, the measurement of time became a formality and a necessity. Research the many ways in which people have measured and recorded time throughout the ages. Go as far back as you can and end your research in the present.

8. Consult an encyclopedia under the subject heading "Time" and look for a chart or explanation of World Time Zones. Record the differences in clock times between the U.S. and your country of origin at 8 a.m., 12 noon, 6 p.m., and midnight. If you were a world traveler, would it be possible to lose a day or pick up a day in your travels? Find the answer in your study of the world time zones. Explain.

NAME _____

DATE _____

PURPOSE: To understand and appreciate the design of calendars which not only measure time but also reflect the variations in the life of a cultural group.

1. On the back, list the persons you interviewed. Also list books, magazines, pamphlets, family documents and any other sources used for information.

2. THE MOST EXCITING THINGS I LEARNED:

HOLIDAYS

Chapter 7

"If all the year were playing holidays,

to sport would be as tedious as to work..."

Shakespeare

Henry IV, Act I

54

Holendays

The word "holiday" is a combination of two old English words, "holy" and "day." Despite the spiritual tone in the derivation of "holiday," the word is used today to describe any declared day of rest or celebration. Holidays can be quite frivolous or very serious. A number of cultures have specially designated holidays to remember the dead. Such holidays are usually serious -- even somber. There are joyous holidays to celebrate planting time and those for harvest time. Historic events, such as a country's day of independence, are occasions for a holiday. Significant historic leaders will have their birthdays memorialized through a holiday. In most every culture, there is a holiday for the beginning of the new year. Here are some holidays celebrated in America.

APRIL FOOL'S DAY	MARDI GRAS
ARBOR DAY	MARTIN LUTHER KING, JR.'S, BIRTHDAY
CHRISTMAS	MAY DAY
COLUMBUS DAY	MEMORIAL DAY
EASTER	MOTHER'S DAY
ELECTION DAY	NEW YEAR'S DAY
FATHER'S DAY	ST. PATRICK'S DAY
FLAG DAY	THANKSGIVING DAY
GROUNDHOG DAY	UNITED NATIONS DAY
HALLOWEEN	VALENTINE'S DAY
INDEPENDENCE DAY	VETERANS DAY
LABOR DAY	WASHINGTON'S BIRTHDAY
LINCOLN'S BIRTHDAY	

It appears that in every culture there is a recognition of the human need to stop ordinary, daily activities to celebrate, to commemorate, or to make merry. Along with such declared days of respite, may come rituals, services, parades, costumes, specialty foods, certain games, customs, greetings, etc., which distinguish the holiday. In understanding holidays, we can more clearly understand the culture and its community of people. We can define much about a group by studying its holidays. On the other hand, we may also be struck by the many parallels in holidays across cultures (as in celebrations of the New Year or days of thanksgiving) and can feel the ties with our brethren around the globe.

In addition to the holidays generally observed in America, we have happily absorbed the holidays of other ethnic groups such as the Irish tradition on St. Patrick's Day. When we are fortunate to live in neighborhoods which enjoy a mixture of people, we celebrate and participate in each other's special days. If you were Greek living in a Polish neighborhood, you would be welcome to share in the fun of "Dingus Days." These are days which follow Easter. Part of the observance includes playful pranks practiced by young men and women designed to attract attention and be humorously vexing. The laughter is followed by a pleasant repast of refreshments and goodies.

Student Activities

1. In a whole class discussion, brainstorm for all the holidays and commemorative days in existence in the USA. With each contribution, explore the nature of the day, how it came to be celebrated, and the ceremonies which surround it. Select a day of your choice to research. In a few days, share what you have learned.

2. Select an ancestral country to research for holidays and commemorative days. Create a holiday scrapbook for the country with each page devoted to a different holiday. Each page should contain an illustration capturing the spirit of the day as well as relevant information: name of the day, dates on which it is celebrated, the reason for its celebration. The pages should be arranged in chronological order.

3. Select three of four holidays which you want to research in some depth. List a reasonable set of questions which you want answered. A representative sample might be:

> What is the name of the holiday?
> When is it celebrated?
> When was it established?
> What does it commemorate?
> Why is its celebration important?
> Are special ceremonies a part of this day?
> Are there special events?
> What kinds of foods are prepared?
> What greetings are exchanged?
> Are there special costumes, masks or adornments worn?
> Are there special games played on this day?

4. Choose holidays from an ancestral country which have parallels in some other country, for example, Christmas in Mexico and Christmas in Sweden. For each holiday write one paragraph which captures the similarities between the two countries and one paragraph which describes the differences. Such comparisons can also be communicated very effectively through charts.

5. Select an ancestral country for which you will design a colorful holiday calendar. Identify each of the holidays or commemorative days celebrated by that country.

6. Invite a resource person from the community to demonstrate a holiday feature of some country to the entire class. This may be a demonstration by a Ukrainian person of intricate egg painting, called pysanky, at Easter time; it may be teaching a folk dance, a game or a holiday song.

7. Which American holiday is your favorite? Which ethnic holiday is your favorite? Write a paragraph explaining the reason for your choices.

8. Special events take a great deal of planning, thought and cooperative effort. The smoother the plan, the easier it all appears to be to the participants. Select an American or ethnic holiday of your choice. Prepare a program -- a schedule of events, speakers, games, booths for your neighbors to enjoy! Include enough detail so that anyone reading your program will understand the day's plan from beginning to end. Feel free to invite enough entertaining performers and celebrities to make the festivities really appealing.

9. As a class read about holidays and festivals in other countries which sound like fun and would lend themselves to interesting illustrations. Create advertising posters which are eye-catching and colorful to be used as announcements for the upcoming events. Don't be afraid to choose from some holidays which are not well-known! (Find out about Mardi Gras celebrated by Americans of all ethnic backgrounds in New Orleans. This will give you clues to how gala such events can be.)

NAME _____

DATE _____

PURPOSE: To understand the meaning and purpose of my holidays as well as those celebrated by people in every culture.

1. On the back, list the persons you interviewed. Also list books, magazines, pamphlets, family documents and any other sources used for information.

2. THE MOST EXCITING THINGS I LEARNED:

ETHNIC FOODS

Chapter 8

I am yours to be wooed

Great cooks of the world
Their kitchens all humming
A medley of foods
To my stomach they're strumming

Aromas do billow
Tasty clouds are on high
Fragrance and spices
Float hot to the sky

I am captured ----imprisoned
My palate aquiver
A mouth full of joy
Their goodies delivered

I am yours ---- you have won
I have gorged --- I have eaten.
My hunger deployed
            Belly up
                I am beaten!

                G. Lipson

Ethnic Foods

We all know that food is one of the primary needs of all living things since it furnishes the basic fuel--the energy for life and growth. However, food plays another role in human society which goes beyond nurture and survival. Food, rich in symbolism, stands for love, for comfort, for hospitality and for celebration. There is a ritual which surrounds eating at home and in restaurants with families and friends that transcends the "breaking of bread." As an offshoot of this, the art and science of food preparation and presentation is a full-time vocation, profession, or hobby which occupies many cooks on levels of pure aesthetic achievement.

Nowhere is the rich multicultural fabric of our country more obvious than it is in ethnic foods. Standing at any "deli" counter, one can enjoy with one long sweep of the eye, foods from a dozen or more countries. There are Syrian and Greek breads, Italian salads, German braunschweiger, Polish pierogi, Spanish olives, Swiss cheeses, French wines, Scottish shortbread, Greek baklava, French veal cordon bleu, Russian chicken kiev, Lebanese stuffed grape leaves, kosher corned beef, Mexican tortillas, Chinese fried rice, and on and on. The staggering variety which abounds in the preparation of foods by all peoples around the world is a tribute to human creativity.

As you and your students explore the area of ethnic foods, you may want to focus your study on three things: (1) those foods which are the most common in the ancestral country itself, (2) those foods from the ancestral country which have been popularized in the USA, (3) those gastronomical delights or elegant specialties which would be considered gourmet foods for the ancestral country.

It is location, custom, religion, and trade which determine eating habits and menus. Such study should help us appreciate how uniquely people express themselves as a community through the use of foods, spices and herbs.

Student Activities

1. Make a list of foods familiar to you which have their origins in another country. Beside the food item, list the country you think it represents. Discuss your list and the ingredients, spices and herbs which make your foods unique.

2. As a class, organize an effort to call, write, and/or visit various ethnic restaurants for the purpose of collecting as many ethnic menus and informative place mats as possible. Arrange these in a class scrapbook. Use the Yellow Pages of your telephone book to find ethnic restaurants in your neighborhood.

3. Explore food items in one or more of your ancestral countries. Your report may answer the following questions:

    Which are the most common foods?
    Which is the most popular protein source?
    Which vegetables and fruits are most used?
    Is there a milk source or a different liquid
       food substitute?
    What is the country's equivalent to bread?
    Are there specialty breads?
    Which herbs and spices are used?
    What specialty foods are unique to this country?
    Are there "fun" foods such as snacks or desserts?
    What are they made of?
    How are foods preserved?

4. Select an ancestral country for which you will prepare two menus--one menu will reflect an ordinary family's choices for the meals of the day; the second menu will reflect a holiday menu and the kinds of foods and food specialties which would be served.

5. In your ethnic group are there special tools or utensils which are used? Are there special ways of preparing foods? Is there a special order or style in which foods are served (salad last, fruit and cheese for dessert, cold soup, etc.)? Take good notes and be prepared to discuss these.

6. Invite various resource people to provide cooking demonstrations of special dishes. Such resource people should be able to provide information about the foods, the spices and herbs, and cooking procedures specific to that group. Write letters of appreciation to the resource person following the visit.

7. Pretend that you are inviting friends to dinner. You are going to prepare a multiethnic dinner. Each course will represent a different country. Describe each course from appetizer to dessert. Decorate your menu with appropriate pictures and illustrations. Include a warm letter to your friends inviting them to this ethnic feast.

8. Research foods which had ethnic beginnings but were invented in America. For example, potato chips were invented in 1853 by George Crum, an American Indian chief. Doughnuts were originally a Dutch "oily cake," but the holes were put in (or taken out) by Hanson Gregory in 1847. The ice-cream cone was invented in 1904 at the St. Louis Exposition by Ernest A. Hamwi and was originally a circular Persian pastry. Chow mein was created by Chinese laborers working on the Transcontinental Railroad in America in the 1800's. You may find that your librarian is helpful in locating special reference books which have such information.

9. Here is a poem about foods for you to enjoy and work with.

Win Me with a Regal Charlotte Russe

Wrap me in a grape leaf
crunch me with chitlins
tickle me with tortillas
cool me with vichyssoise
warm me with Welsh rarebit

Ply me with pita bread
seduce me with a pizza
brighten me with beet borscht
coax me with a curry
bombard me with baklava

Taunt me with a trifle
fire me with Szechuan
pep me with paprikash
beguile me with weiner schnitzel
tempt me with sukiyaki

Goad me with gefilte fish
hound me with haggis
console me with corn pudding
josh me with yummy jambalaya

Now--soothe me with a sparkling seltzer, please!*

G. Lipson

*plain carbonated water

With a partner or in a triad, research ethnic foods from international cookbooks and create your own delicious poem. Use imperative sentences as those above. Use alliteration and strong adjectives. Use your combined imaginations as your strongest ingredients. Remember--this is a

poem which does not rhyme. Search out the book entitled EATS by Arnold Adoff for a gastronomic treat with words. What does *gastronomy* mean?

10. Some ethnic recipe books have clever and appealing titles. Look through the card catalogue in the library or through the international cookbook section for some catchy titles such as NOTHING BEETS BORSCHT by Jane Blankstee or FILLINGS WITH FALAFIL, or LIKE MAMA USED TO MAKE. List these titles. Now make up some of your own catchy titles for a tasty cookbook of your own. What delicious sounding ethnic recipes have you encountered which you would like to try? What are the names of these recipes?

11. Name the kinds of ethnic candies and sweet treats enjoyed by your family such as halvah, marzipan, taiglach, chrusciki, or lokoom, etc. Describe them and include as many ingredients as you know which go into their preparation.

12. The tomato originated in South America. It was cultivated in Mexico by American Indians and introduced in Europe in the 16th century. It was thought to be poisonous because it was related to the poisonous mandrake and belladonna plants. It was a daring moment when Robert Gibbon Johnson performed the historical feat in 1820, of eating a tomato in public view on the courthouse steps in Salem, New Jersey--*and stayed alive.* Research a food and write a human interest article on such an event. Include the 5 W's of journalism--"who-what-where- -when-why (and sometimes how)."

NAME _____

DATE _____

PURPOSE: To appreciate all the joyous variety of food and the ethnic creativity expressed in its preparation and presentation.

1. On the back, list all the persons you interviewed. Also list books, magazines, pamphlets, family documents and other sources used for information.

2. THE MOST EXCITING THINGS I LEARNED:

Chapter 9

FOLK MEDICINE AND SUPERSTITION

"Ate an apfel /afore gwain bed/
makes the doctor/ beg his bread."

An Olde English verse

(An apple a day keeps the doctor away.)

Folk Medicine and Superstition

FOR THE TEACHER

Throughout civilization, people have demonstrated a strong inclination to deal with the vagaries of fate. This is nowhere more apparent than in confronting illness and disease--thought to be the machinations of the devil. It is equally apparent in the desire to ward off evil events or to encourage good ones. Out of such human inclination has come the rich mixture of folk medicine and superstition.

Medicine, historically, was tied to magic in its very beginnings. Indeed, the art of healing was regarded as a special branch of magic. In Europe in the 15th century, in addition to the invocation of magic, people had begun to use herbs as medicine to cure their ills. Folk medicine refers to the old-fashioned remedies used in the substances of every kind. These techniques were used by the common people and handed down through the centuries from their ancestors. Folk cures, in all their amazing variations, are indigenous to all cultures. Some of the very first books printed in Latin, English and German around 1440 included information about the healing properties of some plants and the appropriate prayers and chants to be sung while using them.

It is true that every culture in the world has a collection of bits and pieces of old wives' tales, assorted bits of psychological and quasi-medical information, cures, and preventatives. What is even more astonishing is that some of the cures really worked, particularly those which had to do with the ingestion of substances. These remedies were sometimes scientifically sound, though no one could give the reasons why they worked. For example, chicken soup, of late, has enjoyed a new respectability because of the scientific affirmation that it does, indeed, have helpful qualities.

A strange, old practice worthy of mention was one intended to transfer the illness from a human to another living creature or an object. A fish, an animal or a tree might serve this function quite well. For example, if a child were suffering from whooping cough, his parents might stuff his mouth with a young frog. They would then toss the hapless amphibian into the garden where they expected him to cough his little heart out, having had the child's cough transferred to him. Another transfer technique requires the use of a live chicken. The unsuspecting fowl was to be swung round and round, over the head of the ailing person, to the accompaniment of the proper prayer to effect the transfer cure.

In our modern sophistication, we may laugh at the suggestion of the London dentist who wrote to the LONDON TIMES during the great cholera epidemic in 1832. He suggested that the government place cannons all over the city and fire them off every hour to "disinfect the atmosphere." It was a perfectly acceptable notion of the times that if the atmosphere were disturbed, it would cause the fatal airs to disperse.

The subject of folk medicine leads inevitably to superstitions--a body of nonscientific beliefs and attitudes which people observe out of ignorance and fear. Superstitions began in primitive times, when humans, who had very little control over their lives, tried to find reasons for things that happened to them. If these occurrences were bad, they tried to avoid them in the future. If they were good happenings, they wanted them to happen again! Because this is so understandable in human terms, there is not a culture which has been free of superstition.

While we are no longer primitive, and we certainly understand more about the natural world, many superstitions persist. We hang on because, as much as we laugh at some of these beliefs, we are really trying to be on the safe side and not tempt fate. We have the benefit of more education and modern science, but we still do not have control of chance, of events, of probability, fate,--or whatever one wishes to call it. Perhaps it is this that makes us wish desperately for more control by observing little superstitions. We knock on wood, throw salt over our shoulders (to hit the devil in the eye), avoid black cats, make a wish with a chicken bone, distrust number 13, walk around ladders, and try not to break mirrors with their promise of seven years of bad luck.

There are superstitions for every occasion and every field of human endeavor. We see expressions of it in sports, music, theatre, medicine, love, marriage, and the weather. The list goes on and on, full of mystery and funny magic.

Student Activities

1. Start a "WOULD YOU BELIEVE" bulletin board. Contribute to a list of superstitions and folk cures to be displayed on the board. How many can you think of, have you heard of, or read about? (Knock on wood, fear of Friday the 13th, cures for warts, wearing amulets, etc.)

2. Ask your parents or grandparents if there were special remedies they remember being practiced in your family for sore throats, earaches, toothaches, coughs or colds. What experience have *you* had with a home remedy used by your mother which you think helped you? List each of these remedies, their ingredients and how you think they helped.

3. Many people of different cultures believe in the power of the "evil eye" which brings bad luck or illness. All groups deal with it differently. In the old days some people wore amulets of glass beads, little sacks containing ingredients or other objects around their necks to ward off trouble. Some still utter expressions to keep bad luck away. What good luck charms do you know about? Have you ever had your own good luck charm? What anti "evil-eye" techniques or expressions are used in your cultural group? Write each of these on a separate card and share them with your classmates. Perhaps other classes would be interested in your findings. Collect as many as you can. Choose an editorial committee to select some of the most interesting of these items. Illustrate them on large construction paper with the written information. Display these outside the classroom.

71

4. In the old days, some medicines were given to people as a general cure-all. There were castor oil, sulphur and molasses, and other tonics. There is a long list of such nostrums in the history of "patent medicines." Find out what the term "patent medicine" means. Investigate to find commercial names of some of these medicines. Were there favorites used by your family which are still remembered? What are they? A funny example of truly bogus medicine was "Comet Pills" which were on sale in 1910 and were intended to protect people when Halley's Comet was to pass close to the earth in that year. What would an advertisement for "Comet Pills" look like? Design an ad complete with slogan and illustration.

5. When we mix the curing arts with superstition we learn about people like Indian Shamans who had special powers to cure the sick. Were there people in your ethnic group who took the place of doctors and were respected? What were they called? Discuss your findings and the reason why the services of such people were used. What kind of training did they have?

6. In early America there were medicine men who peddled their "snake oil" from town to town in horse drawn wagons. They put on shows to attract attention and then sold their wares to people standing in the audience. How were these peddlers similar to commercial hucksters on TV? With a small group of classmates, write a series of TV commercials using old time medicines or ethnic cures! Perform these skits for the class.

7. Dandelion was used for kidney and liver disorders in the old days. Periwinkle leaves were supposed to help relieve the pains of boils and cramps, and the juice extracted from the mugwort plant was a drink prepared to prevent fatigue. The English foxglove plant is important today in modern medicine as a heart regulator. Investigate the medicinal use of plants which are used today and are scientifically acceptable. Collect them in an illustrated booklet with information about what they are used for.

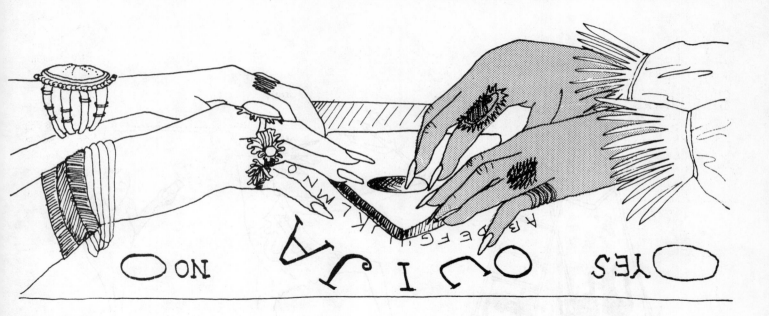

8. We are always intrigued with those people who think they can predict the future. Each has a special way, system or set of props in order to help in such predictions. Some read tea leaves, others use a Ouija board, still others use tarot cards. Find out as much as you can about such people in your cultural group. What are they called? What props do they use? What power do they claim to possess? What are tarot cards which date back to the 15th century and in their ancient form are most magnificent to see? What is a Ouija board? What does it do? What does it mean? Do some research, and choose up pro and con sides to debate the truth of these powers. Keep good notes and be persuasive. (Is there a fortune teller in your class?)

9. Believe it or not, chocolate was first used as a medicine! Find out what chocolate is and where it comes from. Imagine what a delicious experience it could be if it were still used as a medicine. Write a short story to be read aloud to the class about the fun possibilities of such medication. The story is yours to create and the title will be your choice. A few suggestions would be "A Tempting Cure," or "Fun at the Pharmacy," or "Doctor's Orders--Chocolate Fudge with Peanuts Every 4 Hours, Plenty of Fluids and Lots of Rest!"

10. When a person sneezes we say, "Bless you," in English, "Gesundheit," (to your good health) in German, "Salute," in Italian, "Na Zdrowie," in Polish, and "Que Dieu vous benisse," in French. Ancient man was afraid when he sneezed that he had blown his good spirit out of his head and a bad one would move right in. The blessing was to keep the bad spirit out. How do you respond to a sneeze in the language of your forbears? List the many expressions or wishes for good health which are found in your language or the language of others.

11. Even thousands of years ago, numbers were considered to have magical properties. Lucky numbers for the Egyptians were 3, symbolizing the mind of man; 4, for directions (N, S, E, W); and 7, for the house containing the spirit of man. The devil, of course, was associated with unlucky numbers --the most famous being 13, called the "Devil's dozen." Another early belief was numerology, which still has followers. Research this ancient practice and explain how it is supposed to predict your future. Do you know of any other superstitions tied to numbers? Investigate number 9 and its many meanings in various ages and cultures. Are there certain numbers which are special in your culture?

NAME _____

DATE _____

PURPOSE: To appreciate that all people have tried to understand and control the forces which affect their health and the quality of their lives--that superstition and folk medicine are a strong expression of this in all cultures.

1. List the persons you interviewed. Also list books, magazines, pamphlets, family documents and any other sources used for information.

2. THE MOST EXCITING THINGS I LEARNED:

Chapter 10

MEMORIES, NOSTALGIA, ARTIFACTS

" ... the days may come, the days may go,
But still the hands of mem'ry weave
The blissful dreams of long ago."

George Cooper

Memories, Nostalgia, Artifacts

FOR THE TEACHER

Nostalgia describes a kind of homesickness, longing, or yearning for a return to a setting or time in the past. It is a wistful sentimental feeling.

An **artifact** is an object produced or shaped by human workmanship. Tools, coins, pottery, household utensils are all examples. Artifacts of a culture have historical interest and are clues for scholars (such as archeologists) to the way people lived and .worked. The origin of the word is from the Latin--ars (art) and factus (made).

And as for the definition of **memories,** we all know that memories are our entire recollection of things past. Some memories are sweet, some bittersweet, some sad.

The true story on the following pages is intended to be read to your students. It embodies all three dimensions of this chapter--memories, nostalgia, and artifacts.

SHIMMY'S STORY

I was a 14-year-old boy living in Toronto, Canada, in 1932 and everybody called me Shimmy but I don't know where the name came from. (Since there were so many odd nicknames on the street, I suspect they were derived from the native languages of the families and given an English interpretation!) Anyway, my real name is Simon. My parents were Russian immigrants who had 13 children. Our house was connected to another house, side by side, like others on the street, and they were long and narrow. Steps led up to the little gingerbread veranda (porch) and on the door was an ornate twirl bell to ring. You walked into a long, dark hall to the end into a big welcoming kitchen. We had a black cast iron stove which used wood for heat and cooking. It was about 5 feet wide and had deck lids on which pots and pans would cook. There was a mixture of old and new because there was an electric cook stove too.

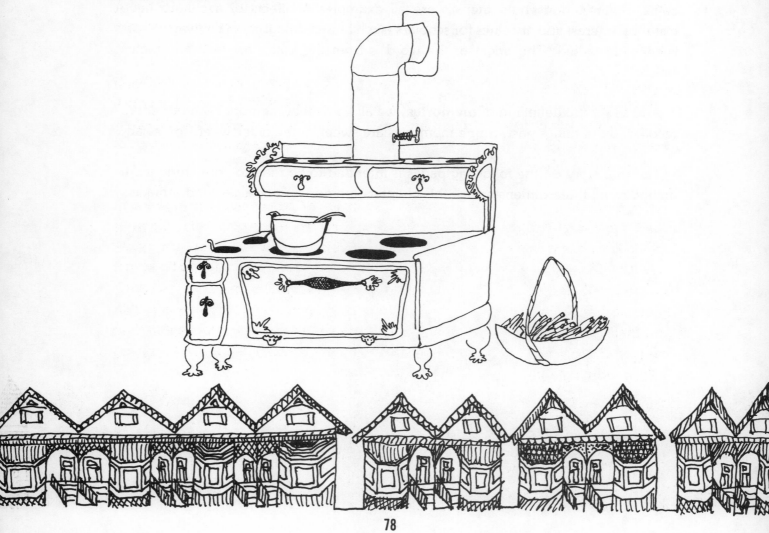

The kitchen was huge and was the most important room because we spent all our time there. There was a big table and lots of chairs and rockers. Even so we ate meals in shifts. We had a big davenport (couch) in the kitchen and that is what made it comfortable. At night, still in the kitchen, the girls in the family did their personal washing in a galvanized metal tub with a washboard and kettles of heated water. They hung their clothes in the "summer kitchen" which was like an enclosed porch with windows connected to the house. This room was also used for food storage and for our pets (always more than one.) We had a cellar which was only used for the storage of coal. It was not a proper room as basements are today.

The parlor and the dining room were closed off by glass doors except for holiday meals and special occasions. It was only used for company but people had to be practically strangers to be considered company and be taken in there. Once in awhile a man would be hired to come into the house to wax all the beautiful oak floors. He used a heavy weight with a soft chamois over it and pushed it with its long handle. He was very powerful, and as we watched him buff and shine the floors like glass, it seemed like terribly hard work.

Our backyard was surrounded by a high wooden fence and was wild and overgrown in the summer with monster sunflowers and giant hollyhocks. (One must see a sunflower to believe it, since it looks like the product of a science fiction experiment!) Nobody did any gardening in back, but the front lawn was a little green grass postage stamp which was always kept neat.

Every morning we kids had a breakfast cup of Fry's Cocoa and sugar mixed with hot water--which we prepared for ourselves from an oversized kettle. Once in awhile someone would eat something different like my big brother Oscar who made cereal with hot milk. We used to call that cereal "frog's eyes," because that's what it looked like. Later, when I was grown up, I learned it was called tapioca. I still don't know how anybody can eat it because it looks so slippery. But Oscar was very thin and that's why he was allowed to have milk and something more nourishing than the rest of us. When we left the house for school we always departed by saying "Good morning," instead of "Goodbye."

My mother worked very hard all day mostly with cooking for our big crew. She was a little fat woman who wore dresses that came down to her ankles and covered the button straps on her flat shoes. Each morning, summer and winter, she took a big heavy shopping bag and walked a far distance to Kensington Market and bought food for supper. When she made cherry pies, which were my favorite, she spread paper out on the kitchen table, took a hair pin out of her hair and pitted quarts and quarts of sour cherries, one by one. We hardly saw my father. He was a pants presser and worked for Tip Top Tailors which was a big company. He worked "piece work." For every pair of pants he pressed he got a job ticket. He counted up his tickets at the end of each day and that's how he got paid. I think he earned 10 cents a pair. He left early in the morning and came home late at night. We all learned from him that everyone could look forward to working very hard to help support the family.

I loved my neighborhood. Every house was different and the outsides were very neat and clean. There were immigrants living there from all over--Italy, Russia, Poland, etc. There was a Maltese family and their origins confused me the most. I couldn't figure out where they came from. But everybody spoke broken English. Sometimes we used words and couldn't figure out where they came from. But they would straighten us out in school. I hated school because it seemed all the teachers were mean. When we practiced handwriting, which was an important subject, anybody who was left-handed was in lots of trouble. We didn't have the kinds of pens that are used today. They weren't invented yet. We used a nib which was metal and was sharp and pointed at the writing end. The blunt end was forced into a wooden holder and the nib was dipped into an ink well in our desk. The ink well was also handy if the girl sitting in front of you had long braids. You could dip the ends of her braids into the well, if you were prepared to pay the price. We were only allowed to write with the right hand. If my teacher walked by your desk and saw you using your left hand, she hit you hard across the knuckles with a ruler. Once I was hit a nasty clout across the ear with a ruler for talking. That ear of mine was sore for a very long time. Nobody from home ever complained--mostly I think, out of

respect for teachers and because they were embarrassed that they couldn't speak English properly. Almost none of the children in my family finished school. They were all expected to go out to work as soon as they could so that they could bring money home to help support the whole family.

The street of my childhood was very narrow but was always busy with horses and wagons and lots of wheels (bikes). Once in awhile a car would come down and cause a big tie-up. Mostly we didn't know anyone rich enough to own a car. Just the sight of one of those modern monsters inching its way down that squeeze of street would always cause a stir of excitement! In the street bustle, of all the peddlers and delivery people who came to the house my favorites were Tony the Italian push-cart banana man, "Pinchu" the Polish iceman, and Charlie the Chinese laundry man. Tony always told us stories about scary spiders he found on his bananas as they lay in his basement ripening. "Pinchu" gave us chips of ice as a treat from the floor of his wagon. He carried a big block of ice on his shoulder with giant metal pinchers sunk into the ice and a piece of burlap on his shoulder to protect him from the cold weight. He would put the ice in the top of the icebox in the kitchen. As it melted, the water would drain down into a pan under the box which had to be emptied throughout the day. Charlie, the laundry man, would come into our kitchen and exchange pleasantries with my mother. Then he would spread a big striped cloth on the floor and fill it with our soiled linens and wrap it with a tight knot. He could carry that big bundle while peddling his wheel back to his laundry store without faltering! Once he let me try it and I fell off the wheel.

An enjoyable place to go was the small grocery store across the lane (alley) from my house. Here we could buy a deliciously rich ice-cream cone for 2 coppers (pennies). Other things we bought were bulk products like milk and oil that came out of spigots (faucets) or tinned (canned) foods. Some foods were in bins, burlap sacks, or in barrels like pickles and processed fish. Other liquid items were dipped from containers with ladles. Everything we bought was purchased on credit. That means our name was in a ledger (a bookkeeping book) and every purchase the family made was entered. If you didn't pay your bills on time and your credit was bad, they stopped selling you groceries.

We played outdoors on the street from dawn to dusk. A most popular game for boys was "puck and stick" which we played in the lane. The puck was like a hockey puck which lay on the concrete. When you hit it properly it flew into the air like a ball and you swung at it with the stick using it like a bat swung with one arm. You would strike it hard and far and then run bases just like in baseball.

Those were my good old days and the warmth of those times will remain in my heart forever. Fifty years later, in 1982, my family homestead was still being occupied. If you would like to see for yourself, it is one of the many houses on Palmerston Avenue, in Toronto, in the province of Ontario, Canada. It remains, as always, a neighborhood of immigrants.

Kensington Market. A series of narrow streets in what used to be Toronto's Jewish community has become, by stages, a cosmopolitan market of amazing variety. Kosher butchers, Portuguese fish mongers, West Indian greengrocers, second-hand dealers and restaurateurs converse in a babel of languages from all quarters of the terrestrial globe. On nearby Spadina Avenue among the Philippine, Korean, Hungarian, Canadian, Jewish and Rumanian stores and restaurants, a wave of Chinese establishments is visible, overflowing from downtown:(Off Spadina, south of College, on Baldwin, Augusta and Kensington.)

Permission of John G. Laschinger, Acting Deputy Minister, Office of Tourism and Recreation, 1982 GUIDE TO ONTARIO, 900 Bay Street, Toronto, ON, M7A 2EI, Canada.

Nostalgia is "heady stuff!" Most of us know the feeling. We have experienced it in those moments when we looked back through old photographs, examined mementoes, rummaged around in the attic looking at old worn utensils, jewelry, clothing and artifacts of all kinds. We sensed the strengthening of our ties with a previous generation, a different culture. Thoughtful scrutiny of such memorabilia provided us with clues about our ancestors' life-styles, their habits, their beliefs.

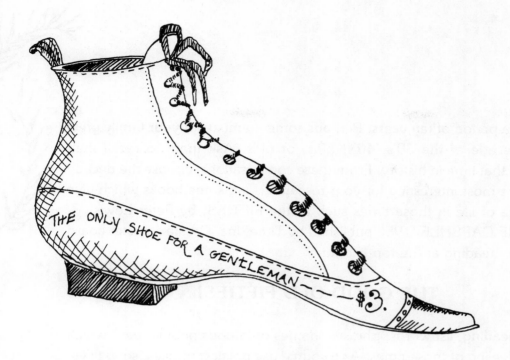

THE ONLY SHOE FOR A GENTLEMAN --- $3.

Student Activities

1.   A mental impression is an image of something formed in one's mind. Take time out to write a list of impressions (or memories) which have stayed with you from your childhood. Let your memory flow. Share these with your classmates. Take the same assignment home to your family. Interview grand-parents, aunts, uncles, or older neighborhood friends. Ask them to recall impressions, memories and descriptions of artifacts. They may remember things like this:

   -a circus wagon
   -bronzed baby shoes
   -sleeping underneath a feather bed (a down-filled blanket)
   -buying fish in a store where the live fish were taken out of a tank to be sold
   -playing jacks
   -crystal set radios made at home
   -wearing gym bloomers
   -making homemade ice cream that tasted salty
   -outdoor plumbing
   -a first pair of high top boots or saddle oxfords
   -a samovar sitting in the dining room
   -a boy's skullsy cap made out of dad's old fedora, covered with bottle caps
   -a votive candle burning in front of a holy picture in the parlor
   -a vintage automobile

2. A decade is a period of ten years. Perhaps some members of your family grew up in the decade of the 30's, 40's, 50's, or 60's. Ask them to recall their memories of that time in history. From these conversations, choose the decade which sounds most interesting for your research. Find some books which give you a picture of life in those times such as the FIFTIES, by Peter Lewis, © 1978 or TIME CAPSULE/1950 published by Time, Inc. Create a poster board with a center heading at the top like this:

THE GOOD OLD FIFTIES!

Under this heading, list words, phrases, names of famous people, etc., which capture the feeling of those times. As a source use politics, movies, song titles, foods, fashions, TV and entertainment which represent that social decade. Illustrate when possible.

PRESIDENTS TRUMAN & EISENHOWER
BILL HALEY & THE COMETS
MARILYN MONROE
I LOVE LUCY
MRS. ROSA PARKS, MONTGOMERY, ALABAMA
THE ATOM BOMB
POPE JOHN XXIII
ROCK 'N' ROLL

3. If you and your classmates were to build a time capsule to capture the decade of your childhood for posterity, what would you include which would help them understand our "modern times"? Make a list on the board of those artifacts you would put in. Remember wearing apparel, books, newspapers, records, movie ads, evidence of food fads, bumper stickers, posters, campaign buttons, toys, etc. What information can you uncover about time capsules which other people have put together in the past?

4. Organize a twenties, or fifties or sixties "Class Dress-Up Day" when everyone must come dressed in the fashion of that decade. Wear the correct hair style when it can be duplicated. Include the teacher and invite any other classes or the whole school to participate, if it is practical.

5. A very important part of our participation in the pride of our people is the need to remember the historical past. There have been (perhaps before you were born) incidents of defeat, sadness and humiliation -- and also chapters of courage, bravery and victory in your ethnic group's history. A culture or a people strive valiantly to overcome those conditions which reduce its dignity. At the same time a group cherishes those events which enhance its selfhood. These times, both good and bad, will live in history forever, but sometimes only engraved upon the heart and not adequately represented in books! Find such an historic time of pride or pain among your people -- understand it, feel it, write about it, share it with your classmates and include it in an honored place in your book on ETHNIC PRIDE. Ask for suggestions at home.

6. Recently, two young sisters, Nancy and Marie, were helping their grandmother move from the old neighborhood. In packing up the furnishings and sweet sentiments of the old homestead, they were thrilled to discover a linen table runner embroidered with yarn the color of jewels, with a story that went back four generations. The thread of the cloth was spun by the grandmother and the cloth was then woven by the great-grandfather. All the embroidery was done meticulously by the grandmother without the benefit of a stamped pattern which was unknown at the time. Stitches were scrupulously counted so that the pattern would look as precise to the eye as the human hand could manage. And the artful designs themselves spoke to the aesthetics of the Polish culture. Find one such item from overseas or America that is cherished in your family and write about it. Include as much information about it as you can for the reader.

7. Compile a chart on which you will list sentimental or valuable items of all sorts which your family owns and which date back to other generations. A chart may include the following categories:

OBJECT	ORIGINAL OWNER	DESCRIPTION
a. wooden whistle	great-grandfather	carved from wood in Bolivia, given as a gift to my cousin
b. a china teacup and saucer		
c. an athletic or scholarship medal		

Ask if you may bring your precious item to school to show and explain to your classmates.

8. Think of some of your own personal belongings at home. Do you have something which you believe could be handed down to the next generation in your family, and could be regarded as interesting and having sentimental value for others? Describe the item and write a futuristic story about *your* children and *your* grandchildren and how they would feel about the artifact you had left them.

9. Select an item about which you have quite a bit of information (a school banner, a great catching mitt, some riding boots, an old copper pot, etc.). Write a short story making the original owner the main character of your story. The item you selected should play an important part in your story. Your story can retell a true event or it can be imaginary. Proofread and edit your story. Switch stories with others in the class.

10. We all need to be reminded that as young people we enjoy or accept some things which may seem very funny in later years. The first line of a hit American song in the 1940's was "Hut-Sut Rawlson on the Rillerah and a Brawla, Brawla, Soo-it." Do you, your parents, or others in your family remember songs or titles from their origins or from America which seem unbelievable? Bring in the information and share. Will the title of any song today seem like foolish madness in the future? Copy the title and the lyrics!

Research on Memories, Nostalgia, Artifacts

NAME _____

DATE _____

PURPOSE: To arrive at an understanding and an appreciation of how a culture expresses itself through its memorabilia, its artifacts and its history.

1. On the back, list all the persons you interviewed. Also list books, magazines, pamphlets, family documents, and any other sources used for information.

2. THE MOST EXCITING THINGS I LEARNED:

Chapter 11

FINE ARTS - FOLK ARTS

MUSIC/DANCE/ART

"The stored honey of the human soul, gathered on wings..."

Theodore Dreiser

Fine Arts - Folk Arts

Fine Arts is the term which describes the expression of trained, gifted and highly refined artists in music, art, dance and the performing arts. The classification may be more inclusive, but it is implicit in the definition that the arts are concerned with "the aesthetic experience." It is not constrained within the parochial limits of a particular region or culture. It takes us into the outer reaches of our intellect to higher levels of appreciation and discernment. The fine arts embody that which is uplifting to the human soul and life-enhancing. It is this aesthetic experience that knows no national boundaries. It is a universal language of beauty which needs no translations. It is a treasure to which all peoples contribute. It endures through the centuries and as such is a window to the past. It makes an historical statement of the times in which it was created. It is produced by the few among us endowed with the powerful gift of talents. These artists seek to express and share with us their artistic response to the world in all its beauty (and its ugliness). With sight and sound, through art forms, we are helped to open our hearts and acknowledge the riches of the human intellect as we experience its elevation from the commonplace.

Folk Arts include many of the categories in fine arts but are different since they are the works of people who may have had little or no formal training, in the classical sense. Folk artists, in any creative field, are talented everyday people who create a wide variety of popular work for ordinary folks. Folk art is important for many reasons, not the least of which is that it serves as a source of historical information about people and their culture. It reflects social, political, and religious beliefs--and makes a colorful, exciting statement as surely as the Folk Arts reflect a specific culture or region. The categories, however, remain the same and include art, music, dance and the performing arts. The following is a list of just a few of the forms of creative expression to be found in the Folk Arts: musical instruments and folk dances, needlework, decorated signs, weather vanes, stoneware, metal pots, furniture, hand-carved decoys, primitive paintings (see the work of Grandma Moses 1860-1961; Edward Hicks 1780-1849). The list goes on, differing with countries and regions, but it is always an expression of the common people handed down through the generations.

In both Fine Arts and Folk Arts, one need only record the names of favorite musicians, singers, composers, dancers, artists, sculptors and actors to develop a list which reads like an international roster of ethnic names. Whether our tastes are traditional or contemporary--we enjoy the performance of talented people. It can be rewarding to stretch in both directions, to acknowledge the gifted people who have made a creative contribution either in the classical realm (Fine Arts) or popular realm (Folk Arts).

Student Activities

TEACHER: Whether to explore the Fine Arts or Folk Arts activities in this chapter should be guided by the student's interest and choice. One may mix or match in any of the categories provided it is meaningful for the student.

1. People often have favorite national songs or folk songs which are stirring, patriotic, romantic or just plain fun! Ask older members of your family about the titles of ethnic songs which are special to them. Bring the titles of ethnic songs and early American songs to school. Design a bulletin board with the information.

2. Music is a part of every culture all over the world. It is a social diversion, a part of recreation and play for people. It is a popular activity which is an important part of gatherings, festivals, worship and even war. Many cultures are known for musical instruments which are unique to their culture. Here are only a few of such instruments:

   African thumb piano   Indian sitar
   Alaskan stone flute   Appalachian dulcimer
   Arab kanoon   Russian balalaika
   Chinese moon-guitar   Greek water organ
   Japanese bawas   Italian concertina

   What instruments are common to your culture and your ethnic music? Illustrate the instruments, label them and describe them. Is there someone among your family or friends who can play an instrument which is special to your ethnic group? Extend an invitation to that musician to come to school and play for your class. Do you have any folk music recordings you can share with your classmates?*

---

*The world's largest selection of authentic folk music is available through Monitor Recordings, Inc., 156 Fifth Ave., New York, NY 10010.

3. There are two charming African sayings, both of which come right to the point and make a statement about the joys of dancing. "If the dance is pleasing, even the lame will crawl to it" and "You say you will dance 'till daybreak, but did you ask the drummer?" Each ethnic group has its favorite dance which originated in the homeland. There is the fandango from Spain, the tango from Argentina, the polka from Czechoslovakia, the rhumba from Cuba, the hula from Hawaii, and the bolero from France. In America, Black Americans were responsible for the cake walk, shimmy, turkey trot, lindy hop and countless others. Find the names of the dance favorites of your people. List them. Can you demonstrate one of these dances? Are you able to teach the steps to your classmates?

4. The names of special dances suggest the names of special dancers and choreographers both classical and modern. A famous ballerina, born in 1925, was Maria Tallchief who was part Osage Indian and was brought up on an Indian reservation. She made her debut with the Ballet Russe in 1942. Jose Limon was a dancer and choreographer born in Mexico (1908-1972) and danced until he was an older man. Agnes DeMille, a choreographer of Dutch ancestry, born in 1909, was famous for bringing ballet to Broadway and popularizing it in such famous productions as OKLAHOMA. Do some library research and find the names of both modern and historical people in your ethnic group who have made a contribution to the world of dance. (What is a choreographer?)

5. When we list important musical figures, we draw from a rich ethnic pool--Duke Ellington (1899-1977) was a famous Black composer called "the greatest single talent in the history of jazz." He was a jazz musician and band leader; John Philip Sousa (1854-1932), a Portuguese-American was called the "March King" of the U.S. Marines and wrote "Stars and Stripes Forever"; Dimitri Mitropoulous (1896-1960), a Greek-American symphony conductor; Ignace Jan Paderewski (1860-1941), a Polish pianist, composer and great patriot; Zubin Mehta (1936-), an East Indian-American, Musical Director of the Los Angeles Symphony and the New York Philharmonic; Itzhak Perlman, violinist, born in Israel in 1945 who came to the U.S. to appear in an all-Israeli talent show and stayed. List some names of composers, musicians and conductors from your ethnic group, whether they live or lived in America or in their native country. These musicians may be modern or historical. If you have a record at home or any music performed or composed by a person on your list, bring it in to share with your class. Try to check out some of these records from local libraries or media centers.

6. On July 4, 1831, the song "America" was introduced by Dr. S.F. Smith, a Baptist minister who wrote the words but couldn't write the music. He set the song to the music of the British national anthem, "God Save the King" (which the British had lifted from the Germans)! Can you find a copy of the words and music of the national anthem from your country of origin? Can you translate it with help, sing it, or bring a recording of it to class? National anthems of countries may change when there is a political change but some songs remain as a permanent expression of the people. Has the national anthem of your forbears changed? What is it now?

7. In the Detroit Institute of Arts, there is a vast mural by the great Mexican painter Diego Rivera (1886-1957). It covers four walls and tells a story which starts with the creation of life and technology, the role of the natural elements air and water, the assembly line in the automobile factories and the races of man within that sweeping scene. Rivera's murals, which deal with his favorite subjects of revolution and labor, may be seen in public buildings all over Mexico. Try to discover a famous painting, from the past or modern times, done by a woman or man artist in your ethnic group. Find a work of art with an interesting story. Take notes and prepare to tell the story to the class. In an art book, try to locate a picture of the work to show on an opaque projector. Be sure to take good notes so that your story will come alive for your classmates.

8. All countries and their people have some art form through which they may be popularly known. Polish poster art is a fascinating example of this, as is Japanese origami (the art of paper folding), West African masks and leather goods, Navajo Indian jewelry and Eskimo bone carvings. Find the folk art of your people, describe it and try to find pictures of it or illustrate it. What materials are used? Explain the reason for the choice of those materials.

9. Who are some of the classical, folk, gospel, or popular singers from your ethnic group who have contributed to the musical pleasure of audiences over the years? Think of some such performers such as Justino Diaz--a Puerto Rican-American Metropolitan Opera star; Buffy-Sainte-Marie--a Cree Indian folk singer; Neil Sedaka--A Sephardic Jew who emigrated from Turkey and both sings and composes; Stevie Wonder--a blind, black, gifted singer and composer. Try to find classical, pop, and folk singers from your ethnic group in your search. Listen to some of their songs. Design an album cover. Write a description of the performer(s) for the back of your album cover. Share any records you may have with members of your class on a happy Friday just before dismissal! Put your album covers on display.

10. The Polish American sculptor, Korczak Ziolkowski once worked as an assistant on the Mt. Rushmore memorial. It inspired him to undertake an even more ambitious project. He has been working on a statue of Chief Crazy Horse carved into the Black Hills of South Dakota, since 1951. According to Ziolkowski's projections, the chief's arm will support 4,000 people, the horse's nostril will accommodate a 5-room house, and the feather on the top of the chief's head will be 44 feet tall. By 1982 the sculptor had already removed 5 million tons of rock from the mountain! If you were to memorialize three of your countrymen or women, in a place similar to Mt. Rushmore, who would those people be? What would your reason be for selecting them? What different kinds of sculpture can you discover that have been created by members of your ethnic group? Describe a particular piece, modern or classical, which is noteworthy, because of size, subject or materials? Can you find a picture of it or illustrate it?

11. Explore the world of theater arts (stage, screen, radio and TV). Who are the important writers, actors, radio personalities, TV performers, film makers, directors, etc.? Who are some of these great personalities from your ethnic group? They may be people who have achieved fame in their native countries or here in America. Make a circle chart and divide it into as many pie-shaped pieces as you have categories. On each pie-shaped piece write the name of the category and include all the names of those personalities who are known for their contribution.

12. Pretend you are a critic for a local newspaper. Write a "rave" review in praise of the performance of a single performer or an ensemble of people from your ethnic group. How would your review express something admirable about the talent this group might display? Create a name for the show and the troupe. Here is a quote which will serve as an example:

"Black voices tend to be very mellow, very rich, and very dark, so that even in the upper register there's always that delightfully sfumato (smoky) quality. There's a real intensity of emotion that gets displayed no matter how light or festive the feeling. There is a glimpse of the soul, I think, that comes forth in every note whether it's anguish or sheer joy that's being displayed."

M. Barry Alexander, Black Lyric Tenor
MONTHLY DETROIT MAGAZINE

NAME _____

DATE _____

Research on Fine Arts and Folk Arts
Music/Dance/Art

PURPOSE: To become aware of the very special and unique contribution my ethnic group has made to the world of Fine Arts and Folk Arts, through the centuries.

1. On the back, list all the persons you interviewed. Also list books, magazines, pamphlets, family documents, and any other sources used for information.

2. THE MOST EXCITING THINGS I LEARNED:

Chapter 12

LANGUAGE

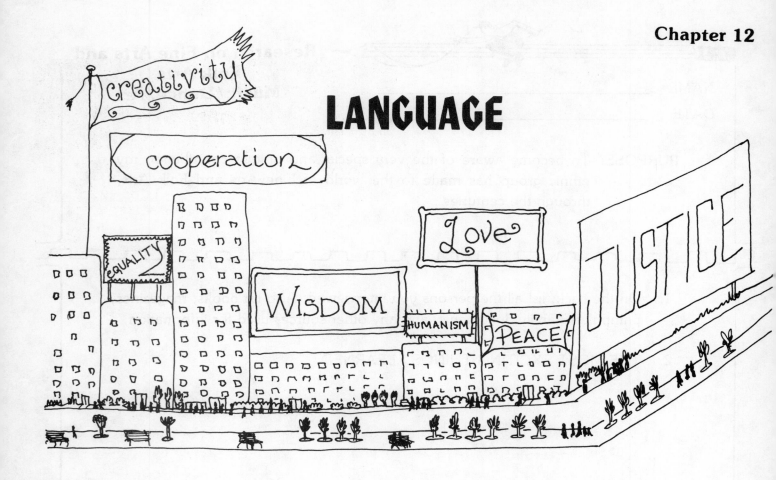

Words:

"They sing, they hurt. They teach.
They sanctify. They were man's first
immeasurable feat of magic. They liberated
us from ignorance and our barbarous past."

Leo Rosten

Language

Perhaps the most significant of all human behavior is that of communication through a language. In a miraculous quantum leap, language sets us apart from the animals. It provides us with the medium through which we establish a civilized society and offer one another the gift of culture, knowledge and history, in perpetuity.

Language is like a living organism -- constantly evolving and changing. It responds to needs, to new ideas, to changing technology. To demonstrate this, it would be simple to compile a list of words in use today which were nonexistent years ago. Because language is so dynamic, people constantly change it and adapt it to suit their purposes. It has always been a fact that language is a mirror of people and places. The same language may have various regional aspects which we call dialects. A dialect of a language is characterized by features of vocabulary, grammar, pronunciation, and even, at times, social class. Some language experts claim that there are over 2700 separate languages and over 5000 dialects in the world today. Of these, there are approximately 400 known writing systems dating back to the first alphabet conceived by Phoenicians around 1000 B.C.

Language not only reflects reality but also orders that reality and is therefore a tribute to human creativity. Communication, a basic human need, exists in the most primitive as well as the most sophisticated of societies. Language allows us to deal effectively with our environment, to communicate with others, to express our feelings and ideas, to transmit knowledge and values, to arrive at new understandings, to comfort one another, to love one another and to live our daily lives with some grace. We need only permit language, with all its sweeping beauty and all its power, to enter our world and transform it.

The role of any teacher in any classroom is threefold, according to Bill Martin, Jr. First, the teacher must invest the child's home language with legitimacy; secondly, the teacher must expose children to the *public language* of the larger society; and thirdly, teachers must expose their students to the aesthetic, uplifting *language of literature*.

Student Activities

1. The letters of the A B C's, which we use to represent our language in print, is not used all over the world. Other cultures use their own unique writing systems. Some of these writing systems use very interesting visual symbols which look like works of art such as Bengali, Balinese, Cyrillic, Arabic, etc. Research the various writing forms and find at least 5 different writing systems. Describe as much as you can about each system. Try to print a sample of writing for each one.

2. Etymology is a word which describes tracing the origins of words and their meanings. It is only one of the many fields of research in the study of language. Browse through an English language dictionary. Find at least twenty words whose origins are from another language. Record the words and their countries of origin. Include the spelling of the word in its original language as it is recorded in the dictionary.

3. What does the numbering system look like and sound like in the language of your ancestors? Do the numerals look different? How about the number words? Make a chart to show the English numerals and number words as well as their counterparts in another language. Here is a sample:

ENGLISH	SPANISH
1 - one	1 - uno
2 - two	2 - dos
3 - three	3 - tres
4 - four	4 - cuatro
5 - five	5 - cinco
6 - six	6 - seis
7 - seven	7 - siete
8 - eight	8 - ocho
9 - nine	9 - nueve
10 - ten	10 - diez

Learn to say the numbers. Recite them in class.

4. Make several lists for common objects, for example, "Around the House," "Around the School," "Outside." Write at least twenty common items in English for each list. Alongside each English word, write its counterpart in the language of your ancestors. Here is a sample:

AROUND THE HOUSE

ENGLISH	ARMENIAN
chair	a-torr
table	se-ghan
dish	aman
bed	maheech
cat	gadoo
mouse	moog
dog	shoon
house	doon

5. In 1721, James Kelley said, "Meat feeds, cloth clothes, but manners make the (person)." What is your interpretation of that statement? Choose a partner with whom you will work on the following project. Write a brief, one-page, creative skit in which you try to include as many expressions of courtesy as possible. As you perform this skit before your classmates, challenge them to record as many of these cordial remarks as they hear.

6. Every language and culture has courteous ways of dealing with life situations. Such greetings and polite sayings help us all live more peacefully and more gracefully with one another. Can you find the counterparts for these sayings or language expressions in one of your ancestor's languages?

ENGLISH	ANCESTRAL LANGUAGE
Hello	_____
Good-bye	_____
Please	_____
Thank you	_____
You're welcome.	_____
Good morning!	_____
Good night!	_____
Excuse me.	_____
I'm sorry.	_____
I love you.	_____
Yes, please.	_____
No, thank you.	_____

7. In language, just as in clothes, there are fads and fashions. What words or phrases are currently popular with you and your friends? Which ones of these do not seem to make any sense at all? Find some of these expressions from America's past and present like "23 skidoo," "And away we go," "Like, man…," "Ya know…." Write as many as you can, using one card for each slang expression. Collect them from your classmates and mix them in a container. Have one volunteer at a time pick a card and act out a situation in which that expression can be used. If you're not sure, put the card back and take another.

8. Choose one of your ancestral strands. Pretend you have a cousin who lives in that country. Write the cousin a brief invitation to your birthday party. Write it in English first. Have someone at home or in your neighborhood or school help you translate it into the language of your ancestors. Copy it in your best handwriting, decorate it, and share it with your classmates. Point out the kind of alphabet or characters which are used and the direction in which it is read. Learn to read your invitation.

9. All cultural groups are fortunate to have people of letters--authors, playwrights, writers, and poets--among them. These people have the talent to present their culture to the rest of the world. The Americans had William Saroyan; the Jews, Bashevis Singer; the Blacks, Maya Angelou, etc. Investigate writers representing your ethnic group. Discover the kinds of things they have written and share the pride of their achievements in a one-page autobiographical statement--as if you were the person who represents the soul of your culture.

10. Is there a poem, lullaby, finger play, or song that is very popular in the language of one of your ancestors? English nursery rhymes, like "Patty-cake," or popular songs, such as "Hail, Hail, the Gang's All Here," are common in the experience of those growing up in America. What would be popular in your ancestral country? When is such a language form used--(poem, finger play, group song)? Who uses it? Can you teach this language form to your classmates?

11. Select a comic strip which you enjoy. Cut out the dialogue balloons from the strip. Now paste the comic strip on a fresh sheet of paper. In each balloon provide your own dialogue written in the language of one of your ancestors. It is not necessary to keep to the English story line as it appeared originally in that comic strip. Get into small groups and be prepared to read and translate your strip into English for your classmates.

12. A proverb is a pithy saying full of wisdom or truth usually expressed in one compact sentence. The language is most often old-fashioned and should express a common experience. It must be an expression which has been in use for a long time to rank as a proverb. Other terms for proverbs are maxims, adages, aphorisms, truisms, mottos, etc. The problem with proverbs, however, is that because they are old, they often may refer to things from the old days which are not familiar to many modern people. Some of the following proverbs may sound strange and may take awhile to work out, but we promise it will provide fun with language and the job will be worth it! Select any three and decide what they mean. Compare notes with your classmates and your teacher. Try to arrive at the real meaning. Here are some all ready to be used and explained:

a. The grass is always greener on the other side of the fence. (What you don't have often looks better than what you do have.)

b. Look before you leap. (Be careful before you decide to do something.)

c. Too many cooks spoil the broth. (Better not have too many people doing one job. They are liable to make a mess out of it.)

d. Every cloud has a silver lining. (Even though things look bad there is usually something good in the situation.)

e. Don't count your chickens before they're hatched. (You cannot always depend upon things to turn out the way you expect them to.)

f. Let sleeping dogs lie. (Don't find fault with other people because you may have faults, too.)

g. Haste makes waste. (A job done too quickly may be so imperfect that it must be done all over again.)

h. All that glitters is not gold. (Everything that looks good is not necessarily good.)

i. People who live in glass houses shouldn't throw stones. (Don't find fault with other people because you may have faults, too.)

j. Don't cry over spilt milk. (It's all over, so forget it.)

13. Compile a "Book of Proverbs" from your ancestral country. List one proverb per page in the original language if possible. Restate the proverb in modern English and provide an illustration to accompany it. A suggested title for the cover may be a quote from the Arabic which reads, "A proverb is to speech what salt is to food."

14. The United Nations building is in New York City. At its meetings are representatives from countries from all over the world. Not everyone speaks English. When a speaker addresses the entire assembly in a language, how do people from other language groups understand what is being said? Find books describing how the United Nations organization works and how this language problem is solved. Share this information with your classmates.

15. FAMILIAR QUOTATIONS, by John Bartlett, was first published in 1882 and includes quotations from ancient authors and those who wrote in foreign languages. It is only one of many books of this kind. Find a quote by a member of your ethnic group which you believe is especially strong, beautiful or meaningful. Write out the quote, explain it, and give your reasons for selecting it.

NAME _____

DATE _____

PURPOSE: To appreciate the color, diversity and power of language--in all forms
of human communication.

1. On the back, list all the persons you interviewed. Also list books, magazines,
pamphlets, family documents, and any other sources used for information.

2. THE MOST EXCITING THINGS I LEARNED:

Chapter 13

FAMOUS PEOPLE

Be not afraid of greatness:

Some are born great,

Some achieve greatness,

and some greatness is thrust upon them.

Shakespeare
Twelfth Night
Act II Scene V

Famous People

Every culture, every society, has its share of creative, talented people who achieve fame. Fame usually implies a favorable quality. For some, fame will be achieved within the cultural or local group alone. For others, it will extend and be recognized around the globe. Some names may be great for centuries, kept alive in history books. Others may be transitory and may not have any meaning in the next decade, but either way, whether the personalities are historical or modern, these people have made their marks. People who achieve "fame" in a *negative* way or through dastardly deeds are said to be "notorious" or to have achieved "notoriety." Every cultural group has its share of notorious citizens, also. This chapter is intended to focus on the positive contributions of a cultural group to the civilized world. It is intended that each student's exploration of famous people will give a heightened awareness of human potential and achievement in every ethnic group.

Every group has been blessed with its share of outstanding women and men who have contributed to our well-being, who have nourished our spirit, who have moved us forward in one way or another. At the same time, it is good to remember that "average" people make their marks, too, through their good citizenship, hard work and daily contributions to the quality of life. It is these "ordinary people" who do indeed assume an important role as models for young people alongside those of great stature.

In developing a sense of identification with your own ethnic group, it can be gratifying to pick out the famous and the great who came from the same roots. This is a way of affirming the contribution of your people. In a very strong way, you feel yourself claiming a share of such achievements with pride. Perhaps it generates other good feelings, too, like the desire to stretch yourself to the fullest and to achieve beyond what you think you can.

In selecting the names of great or famous people--to achieve a pluralistic scope--one must consult sources which truly represent the ethnic group being studied. The perspective of the dominant group in society is the one that is almost always represented in history books. To overcome this limited perspective, we must earnestly encourage the use of ethnic newspapers, ethnic magazines, books and journals written by those who more accurately represent their people. These other voices should be heard in a democratic society.

Creative, talented people can be identified in every ethnic group. Every group has its sages, its problem solvers, its lovers of language, its dancers, its entrepreneurs. There is a pleasant sense of justice in seeing that no one group "has it all."

Student Activities

1. The Nobel Prize was established by Alfred Nobel (1833-1896) who was responsible for the invention of dynamite in 1867. Since he was anxious that his name be associated in history with something other than death and destruction, he established a fund with 9 million dollars which was designed to acknowledge great men and women of achievement the world over. The first award was given in 1901, and Americans have won an unusually large number of those prizes. However, the origins of these American Nobel winners read like an ethnic guide. Many of these accomplished scientists and mathematicians were immigrants to America. This fact stands as a tribute to the mixture of brains and talent which immigrants have contributed to the U.S. Most notable among these awardees was Albert Einstein, a German-Jewish immigrant. He was a physicist and mathematician described as one of the greatest scientists of all time. He won the Nobel prize in physics in 1921.

   Locate a list of Nobel Prize winners in the library for the last five years. Find the names of those winners who are members of your ethnic group. Write down their names and describe the achievements that resulted in their award. In which category did each person win? If you prefer, concentrate your study on American winners only. What is the total number of categories for which the Nobel Prize is awarded?

2. Write some newspaper headlines about the famous feats of your historical ethnic heroes. This classification includes women and men. Analyze newspaper headlines in order to duplicate their style and punctuation. Some guidelines for writing headlines are:

    a.   Compress the information.
    b.   Use the present tense.
    c.   Use your newspaper as a punctuation guide to capitalize your headline.
    d.   Use humor and imagination.
    e.   Don't use articles (the, a, an,) or other words which can be omitted.
    f.   Don't use weak verbs.*

3. In America today, people of every national origin are making significant contributions in every field of endeavor. Look through ethnic newspapers and magazines, such as EBONY, which selects one hundred distinguished Black Americans yearly. Listen carefully to radio and television. Collect articles, pictures, and information about prominent people in your ethnic group who contribute to our national well-being. Develop your own famous people "Ethnic Album."

4. Choose an exciting personality from your ethnic group. Feature this personality in a documentary program which is "on the scene" of the important event in which he/she participated or achieved fame. Assume the role of the commentator. Prepare a question-and-answer script which will uncover information about your celebrity for your listeners. Work with one of your classmates (who will assume the role of the celebrity). Rehearse your program before presenting it to the class.

_____

*EXTRA! EXTRA! READ ALL ABOUT IT!: How to Use the Newspaper in the Classroom, by Lipson and Greenberg, Good Apple, Inc., 1981.

113

5. Pretend that your ethnic hero is the central character in a movie story. The film will be about the life story of that person. The picture is ready to be released, and you must write the advertising copy to attract movie audiences. Read the entertainment section of your local newspaper to learn how it should be done.

6. Pick a famous woman representing your ethnic heritage. She may be alive to-day or she may be from the past. Research her history. Pretend that you are the speech writer for that famous woman who has been invited to deliver an address to a graduating class. You have been told that the speech must be autobiographical in order to inspire other women to train for professional roles in our society. Write a two-page speech. What would you tell the graduating class if, for example, your speech was for Elizabeth Blackwell (1821-1910), who was the first woman in America to graduate from medical school in 1849 (with honors) after having been refused admittance to twenty-nine schools? She spent a lifetime fighting prejudice and humiliation in her attempts to open the medical profession to women.

7. Design a word search like the example shown. Use the names of famous women and men in your ethnic group. The names which are hidden should be listed below the box as clues. This word search contains some of the careers in which you will find famous people.

```
B M G S A L M U S I C B G W K R B E
A U L I T E R A T U R E P E O P L E
T G S P O R T S J O U R N A L I S M
R F R I P Q N E C J H P H Y S I C S
A I J D N M E D I C I N E G K D C B
C H O P T E A C H I N G H O G C B H
K H T J S F S D S C I T I L O P K D
A S E H G P E S S C N I L O P I J F
O J L L E S A D O G D H N H T A M I
G K E M D A N C E E U I W C S T P S
I S I V O F F T C E D S J Z Y R U V K
N T S W R S V W E Z R V U P H E R O
G O I M I L I T A R Y P T Q M X A N
H W O X F A M O U S C B A T Z R X R
S E N G I N E E R I N G S L T R Y S
```

Hidden information appears forward, backward, up, down, or diagonally. Find each word and box it in.

a. business   f. medicine   k. sports   p. music
b. industry   g. teaching   l. politics   q. art
c. law   h. theatre   m. dance   r. space
d. psychology   i. literature   n. engineering   s. physics
e. math   j. television   o. military   t. journalism

8. Work with a partner on this project. Each of you will select a famous person representing your ancestry. That person can be alive today or may be from the past. Be sure you know all about this person's accomplishments. Teach your partner everything you can about this man or woman. Using this information, your partner will construct an object to symbolize that person's achievements. For example, a miniature grand piano made out of cardboard could be an award to a famous musician; or a miniature paper telescope for an astronomer would be appropriate. Your partner will also write a short speech which will be used to present this symbol of achievement. You will now pretend to be that famous person and accept your award as it is presented to you by your partner before the whole class. Be sure to have a short acceptance speech ready. Now switch roles and do the same for your partner and his/her famous person.

9. Talk to your parents, relatives, and friends. Ask everyone with whom you speak to name famous people throughout history who represent your ancestral roots. For every category of work, decide on a color for a construction paper circle which you will use for a collage. For example, artists' names will be on blue circles; sports figures will be on green circles; scientists will be on yellow circles. Print the names boldly in a variety of handwriting styles on the circles. Now, arrange your circles in a unique collage on poster board. Be adventurous--experiment with various color arrangements which are pleasing to the eye. Title your collage to identify your ethnic group. Display in the halls for everyone to enjoy.

10. We all know how to play Fish or Rummy! Use the rules of these games for an ethnic card game. Get into groups of six. Each person will make 3 sets of famous person cards. A set will consist of 3 identical cards. *For example*: student 1 will have:

       3 cards with a famous artist's name
       3 cards with a famous musician's name
       3 cards with a famous author's name
          (the class may decide on the categories)

Each card should include the famous person's name, field or profession, and ethnic group. The famous people must represent the student's ethnic background. When all the cards are put together in a deck, there will be a deck of 54 cards. Shuffle well, distribute according to the rules of Fish or Rummy and enjoy. The winner is the first to get rid of all his/her cards by collecting the sets of 3 and laying them all down.

11. Write an acrostic poem for a famous person of your choice who represents your ethnic group. To write an acrostic poem you will write your celebrity's name vertically down the page using one line per letter. For example: Cesar Chavez (1927---) is a Mexican-American who became a migrant worker at the age of 10 years old when his family lost their farm in Arizona. He attended thirty elementary schools and did not finish eighth grade. Later, as a union organizer, he became an active supporter of nonviolent action to help the conditions of his people, who were migrant farmworkers. He said that the "truest act of courage, the strongest act of manliness, is to sacrifice ourselves for others in a totally nonviolent struggle for justice."

<blockquote>
Chicano power--Mexican American
Every one knows him as a
Supporter of the cause of migrant workers
Always working for the
Rights of free people.
</blockquote>

<blockquote>
Cesar Chavez -- a hero to many
Has a fire inside him
As he fights for justice
Viva la causa! Viva La Raza!
Each person answers his own conscience.
Zealous and fervent in a social cause.
</blockquote>

G. Lipson

Write several phrases for each letter which are descriptive of the person or the accomplishments. Use imagination and powerful language. Out of all the phrases you have written, select those which fit best together. Use only *one* phrase per letter. Do not create a rhymed poem! Be more concerned about capturing the spirit and impression of the person.

12. You want to have a day named in honor of a person in your ethnic group who lives in your community or anywhere in the United States. Write a letter to the mayor of your city or the governor of your state or the President of the United States proposing that this worthy man or woman be honored. Your letter will have to be specific in praise of your candidate and you will need to use persuasive language to sell your point of view. The person for whom you want the holiday named may be politically active, a great teacher, a community leader or a humanitarian.

13. The Pulitzer Prize is a very famous yearly award given in the United States for outstanding achievement in journalism, literature, music and drama. This famous prize, first awarded in 1917, was established by Joseph Pulitzer, a newspaper publisher who founded the **St. Louis Dispatch.** The Pulitzer Prize is acknowledged as a great honor, and many distinguished ethnic Americans have won the prize. Find the categories of awards in the encyclopedia. Write down the categories for the awards. Read the rules for each category. Can you discuss them? Do you think they are fair? What happens if the advisory board does not think that a work which has been nominated is worth the prize? Can you discover whom, among your ethnic group, has won this world famous award?

14. In the library look in the card catalogue for the traditional literature of your ancestors. Read folk tales, myths, tall tales, epics and ballads. Select the story from your ancestral country that has a main character who truly captures the imagination. Read the story carefully and tell the story to the class. You may find different versions of the same tale coming from other countries!

NAME _____

DATE _____

PURPOSE: To discover outstanding women and men in my ethnic group, both in the past and present, who have made contributions to the world community and who enjoy the admiration and respect of many.

1. On the back, list all the persons you interviewed. Also list books, magazines, pamphlets, family documents, and any other sources used for information.

2. THE MOST EXCITING THINGS I LEARNED:

Chapter 14

GAMES AND TOYS

" ..... to love the game beyond the prize."

Sir Henry Newbolt

Games and Toys

It is not hard to believe that games and toys have been around since the beginning of civilization. The oldest board game known now resides in the British Museum. It was last used 4500 years ago in the Sumerian city of Ur -- the biblical Ur of the Chaldees. What is more, the art carved on Egyptian tombs around 2500 B.C. reveals board games and players. The first book of games was compiled in Europe in 1283 A.D. by King Alfonso, the monarch of Castile. He was a brilliant man and he commissioned a group of scholars to produce a series of books on the most important subjects of the day. **Gamesplay** was among those topics recorded. King Alfonso stated that "God has intended men to enjoy themselves with many games (to) bring them comfort and dispel their boredom."

Throughout history there have been three basic kinds of games: games of luck, skill, and physical endurance. Some ancient and modern favorites are checkers, chess, horseshoe pitching, billiards, and ball games. Toys, too, have ancient roots. From ancient Egypt came animal toys, pull toys and balls. From China came tops and kites. The ancient Greek and Roman children played with hoops, miniature boats and rocking horses (shades of the Trojan Horse, perhaps).

To appreciate the sweep and universality of games, one must really have the treat of looking at a definitive work, grandly illustrated, entitled GAMES OF THE WORLD, edited by Frederick V. Grunfeld, copyright 1975, Holt, Rinehart and Winston. The hundreds of illustrations, photographs and diagrams are from research in sixty countries and represent such varied people as Arctic Eskimos, African Tribesmen, the Maori of New Zealand, Tibetan children and American youngsters.

The universality of games is very much evident in the finger and string game called Cat's Cradle. These string patterns have found their way across cultures and thousands of miles, yet we find identical patterns produced in every culture. Equally intriguing are the names of games such as Shove, Ha'penny, Nine Men's Morris, Shogi, Yote, Fox and Geese, Dreidel, Knuckle Bones, and Conkers. Many of the games require that something be made as part of the play. An example of this is Pelele, an ancient party and festival game played in Spain, in which a human-looking stuffed dummy is tossed in the air by young women who launch the body furiously over and over again from a blanket held by the group. The experts explain that this "game" was the way that girls vented their resentment against male arrogance in a dominating machismo society. One may easily recognize many of the games as being more than just child's play.

A brief survey of games reveals international diversity. Badminton originated in India and was named later by an English Duke who loved the game and named it after his estate. Handball was an Irish national sport but was called Fives because it took all five fingers to smack the ball against the wall. Bowling came from Germany and was originally a religious rite. Knocking down the "heidi" or "heathen" was the point of the game. Who would suspect that Tug-of-War, with which we are all familiar, was intended to be a dramatization of the eternal struggle between good and evil. Hopscotch, too, has religious beginnings. It was related to the fascination and symbolism of the maze which represented the sometimes tortuous journey of the soul between life and death. Games and toys have a common character across the world because of their ancient roots and universal implications. This is also true of so many of our life patterns.

Saudi Arabia

Tanzania

Bolivia

Algeria

Student Activities

1. At home, explain this chapter on games and toys. Interview as many members of your family as you can. Pay particular attention to the oldest members of your family. Ask each person to describe and name his/her favorite childhood game. Take good notes so that you can describe or demonstrate the game for the class. How was the game played? What was its purpose? How did one win the game? Do your classmates find your game similar to one in their own ethnic group? Discuss the similarities and differences.

2. Is there a favorite game played in your family circle which represents your ethnic group? An old Italian game called Mora requires no materials and is played with hands only. At picnics, or other gatherings, a group of people will get together in a circle. Two of them will put their clenched fists into the circle. These two are the players. All the others are observers who will take their turns later. Each player calls out a number at the same time. Immediately each player thrusts out a number of fingers. If the combined total of fingers equals either one of the numbers shouted out, the shouter then gets one point. If the number does not add up to any number shouted out, no one gets the point. The first player to reach goal--usually 11 points--is the winner. Could you teach the class a simple game from your family's background? Try to play Mora according to these directions.

3. American Indians in the Ojibwa tribe invented the game of Lacrosse which they called Baggataway. The young Indian braves were known to have enormous intertribal games of Baggataway involving 2000 braves out to play tough. It has since become Lacrosse, the national sport of Canada. Find out more about Lacrosse and its rules. Pretend you are a sports commentator observing the opening session of Baggataway or Lacrosse with 200 young men players on the field. Write a script from which you will read to the listening audience as if you were observing the action. Like all sports announcers, use colorful nouns, verbs and adjectives.

4. The four suits in playing cards were designed by the French in 1500. Hearts were coeurs; Spades were pique; clubs were trefle; and diamonds were carreau. Surprisingly, the suits stood for the social classes! Look at a deck of playing cards and decide what suit would represent:

   a. royalty   c. servants
   b. peasants   d. church officials

   Bring an old set of cards to school and paste one or more of each suit on separate pieces of paper. Give each its proper role in life, a name, and some fictional background information. Don't forget villains and good guys.

5. The game Jai Alai came from the Basque region of the Pyrenees, on the border of Spain and France. Judo was invented by a young Japanese man in 1882 for body building purposes. Gymnastics was introduced in America by German immigrants. What games or sports can you discover that have an old country or ethnic origin? Research the history of some of your favorites and share the information with the class.

6. What is your favorite toy or piece of sports equipment? Pretend you are that favorite toy or piece of sports equipment. What interesting and heartwarming or sad stories would you have to tell about adventures? When we write a story of this kind we are using a writing technique called "personification" -- we are making something that is not alive sound, feel and act alive, as if it were human. You may find it easier to write your short story using these story starters:

   Here I am, (an old baseball bat)....
   Let me introduce myself, I am ....
   I dream about....

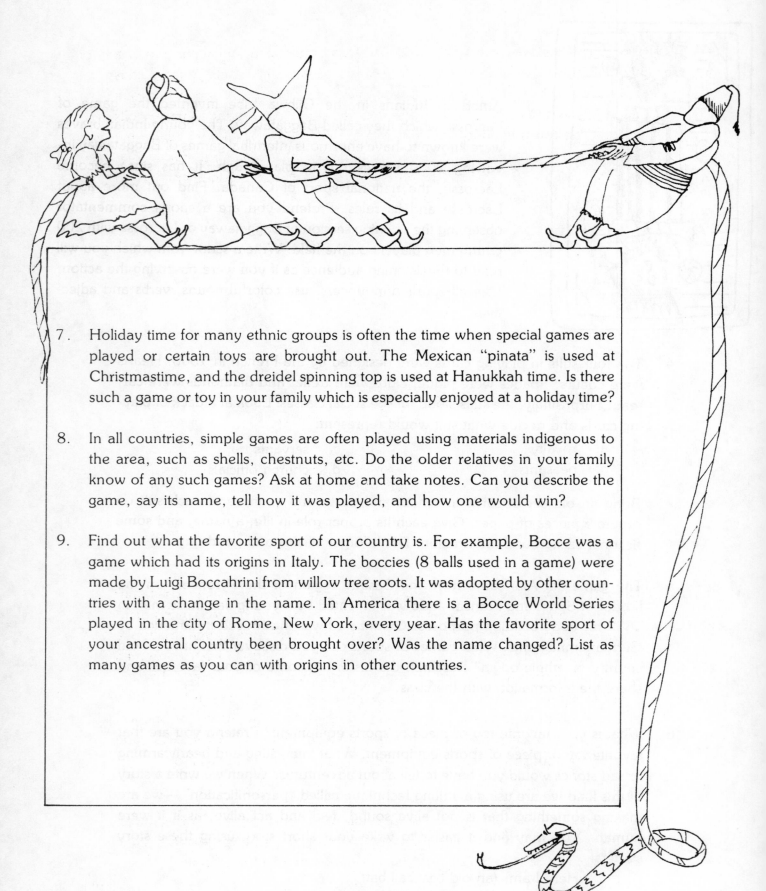

7. Holiday time for many ethnic groups is often the time when special games are played or certain toys are brought out. The Mexican "pinata" is used at Christmastime, and the dreidel spinning top is used at Hanukkah time. Is there such a game or toy in your family which is especially enjoyed at a holiday time?

8. In all countries, simple games are often played using materials indigenous to the area, such as shells, chestnuts, etc. Do the older relatives in your family know of any such games? Ask at home and take notes. Can you describe the game, say its name, tell how it was played, and how one would win?

9. Find out what the favorite sport of our country is. For example, Bocce was a game which had its origins in Italy. The boccies (8 balls used in a game) were made by Luigi Boccahrini from willow tree roots. It was adopted by other countries with a change in the name. In America there is a Bocce World Series played in the city of Rome, New York, every year. Has the favorite sport of your ancestral country been brought over? Was the name changed? List as many games as you can with origins in other countries.

10. There is a fascinating toy which has been around for a long time and is a favorite of Russian and Polish children. It is a traditional "nesting" doll which is made in a set of four or more hollow wooden figures that nest within one another. We see it as one doll, but when it is opened it reveals yet smaller dolls inside. The toy is variously called a Matreshka, or Matryoshka, or Marreshki doll. Many of us have seen it but do not know about the story that is told sequentially as the doll is taken apart. Make this a mystery assignment. Try to locate a set of these dolls and find the story it tells!

Matreshka doll

11. Lincoln Logs was invented by John L. Wright, a Welch American whose father was the famous architect, Frank Lloyd Wright. These logs are toys with notched wooden rails which are used to build log cabins and frontier-type structures. A similar toy is the Erector Set. The inventor, Alfred Carlton Gilbert, observed the actual construction of a high tension tower by a railroad crew. The experience served as an inspiration for the toy with miniaturized parts to replicate real girders, nuts, bolts, etc. The parts are amazingly adaptable for bridges, wheels and whatever the imagination inspires the builder to construct. Can you locate some construction-type toys to bring to class for demonstration?

12. Choose an interesting sport or game of skill and trace its history. For example, the game of chess is believed to have originated in the sixth century in India or China. Some of the names for chess in other countries have been:

CHINA - chong ki   INDIA - chaturanga
IRELAND - fifth cheall   ITALY - sacci alla rabiosa
WALES - tawlbwrdd   SPAIN - ajedrez

13. There is a reason for the international popularity of a game like Monopoly. The game demonstrates the similarity of people's responses to the challenge of buying and selling property. The game was invented by Charles Darrow about 1933 and later was sold to Parker Brothers. Approximately 80 million sets have been sold. The game has been translated for Greek, Hebrew, Portuguese, French, Italian, German, Japanese, Swedish, Danish and Chinese players. Set aside one afternoon dedicated to board games when everyone is invited to bring his/her favorite game to explain and play with in class. Later, have an evaluation and discussion of all the skills required to play some of these games successfully. Invent a board game.

14. A German immigrant named Frederick August Otto Schwarz opened a toy store in the United States in 1870. He called it simply F.A.O. Schwarz. It grew to be the very largest store of its kind in the world and claims to stock some of the most expensive toys in the world. Among other wonders the store is the very largest distributor of stuffed toys -- including life-sized creatures. At one time or another their inventory has included a $10,000 castle-dollhouse, a $7,000 electric train layout, a $2,000 music box, a $700 gasoline-powered scale model car, and life-sized tigers, baby elephants, and five-foot tall giraffes at $1,000 each. Granted any wish you want -- and given free rein in an F.A.O. Schwarz store--describe the adventure you would love to have in this famous toy store!

Information for this chapter derived in part from THE ETHNIC ALMANAC by Stephanie Bernardo, Dolphin Books, Doubleday & Company, Inc., Garden City, New York, 1981.

NAME _____

DATE _____

PURPOSE: To learn about the traditional games and toys of my ethnic group. To understand that humans since ancient times, have enjoyed the pleasure and challenge of these leisure-time activities.

1. On the back, list all the persons you interviewed. Also list books, magazines, pamphlets, family documents, and any other sources used for information.

2. THE MOST EXCITING THINGS I LEARNED:

Chapter 15

HISTORICAL PLACES AND NATURAL WONDERS

HISTORY/TRAVEL/SIGHTSEEING

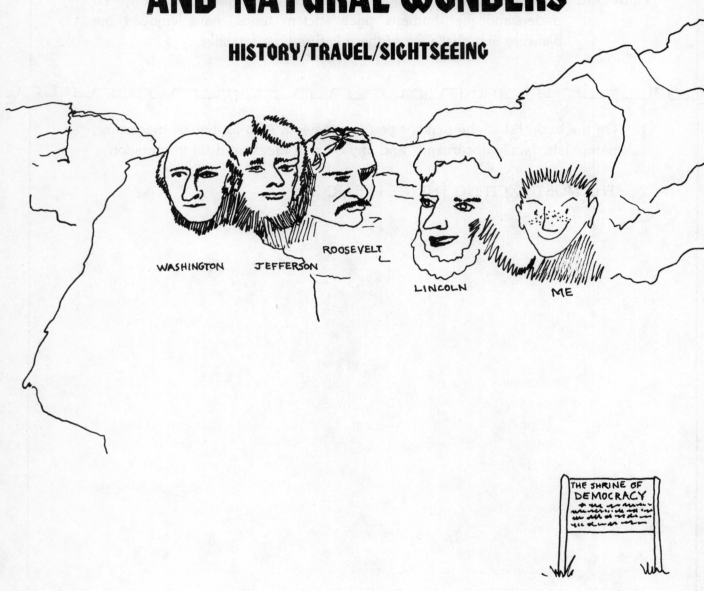

WASHINGTON   JEFFERSON   ROOSEVELT   LINCOLN   ME

THE SHRINE OF DEMOCRACY

"A great spectacle, somewhat resembling the opera."

Bernard deFontenelle

Historical Places and Natural Wonders

FOR THE TEACHER

If we visit the land of our ancestors or travel the vastness of America, we encounter historical places, structures, and natural wonders. These entities have their roots in the mysterious past and stand as awesome legacies in the present.

Hearing about these places cannot duplicate the experience of seeing them. But we do read about them, look at pictures and try to imagine their magnificence. Just as the soul-stirring music of an organ must be heard to be appreciated, so must we actually see the wonders we speak of now in order to perceive their grandeur.

One such awesome sight is the great wall of China--one of the most remarkable engineering feats of all time. It was built by hand in 221 B.C. to keep out invaders. The wall is a winding ribbon of brick and stone which curves over the mountains. It stretches 1500 miles, a distance comparable to that from New York to Omaha. Other such marvels are the great pyramids of Egypt built about 4500 years ago by slaves. These were tombs for mummified kings and were intended to last forever to protect the souls of the monarchs. Each pyramid contained riches and treasures which stagger the imagination.

Nature also provides wonders. The Grand Canyon in northwestern Arizona is one of these. Words cannot describe its magnificence! Its rock formations are millions of years old and each stratum of brilliant color represents an earlier period of time. The colors of the canyon change with the time of day -- red, lavender, gold, orange and green run together in a panoply of heavenly hues.

This topic holds the possibility of painting an extravagant canvas. The students may research the Parthenon in Greece, the Forum in Rome, Mount Fuji in Japan, the Wailing Wall in Jerusalem, the Kremlin of Moscow, the Washington Monument in America, the Gardens at the Palace of Versailles, Angel Falls in Venezuela, the Swiss Alps. They may investigate a grand sweep or a more modest vista!

Just imagine the feeling of being in London, England, and standing on a cobblestone street which was built by the Romans in the first century A.D. These are reflective moments when we contemplate all the monuments of nature and civilization which came before us and all that will follow us. There is, for most of us, a spirit of awe and reverence with which we bear witness to such sights in our travels on this earth.

Student Activities

1. As a group, brainstorm the name of historical places and natural wonders of the world which you have heard about. Contribute to as long a list as the class can manage. Record these on the board. Keep your own list as well. If you have the information, name the country in which each "attraction" can be seen. Are there some countries which have been overlooked? Is your country or region of origin included in the list? Be prepared to add some places to the list which your family has suggested and you would like to visit.

2. You are about to make arrangements for the most spectacular trip of your life to your ethnic homeland! Money is no object! The trip may take one to three months. No one will pack for you; no one will decide what you will see or where you will go. You must take care of all the details, large and small. For this project you may work solo or with a partner, or you may work with a group. Start now, from the very beginning, to outline your grand plan. As a first step decide on major headings and then list the items you must include under those headings. Work with a system--almost as if you were developing a table of contents in your own travel handbook. The organization might look something like this:

I.   MY ANCESTRAL COUNTRY OR REGION OF
     CHOICE (location)

II. TRANSPORTATION ARRANGEMENTS
     a. cost of tickets
     b. schedules - departures and arrivals
     c. time changes
     d. airlines

III. WHAT CITIES WILL I VISIT?
   a. hotel arrangements (or other lodging)
   b. cost
   c. reservation by letter in advance
   d. maps

IV. WHAT HISTORICAL PLACES WILL I VISIT? (description and
     location)
   a. names of places
      landmarks
      impressive structures
      cultural centers
      a national shrine
      an historic cemetery
      historical villages
      a famous birthplace
      museums
      libraries
      bridges
      castles and palaces
      galleries
      monuments
      a house of parliament
      churches and cathedrals
      a battleground
      amphitheaters
      ancient ruins
      period homes
   b. transportation (bus, rented car, bike)
   c. conducted tours (arrangements and costs)
   d. time schedules

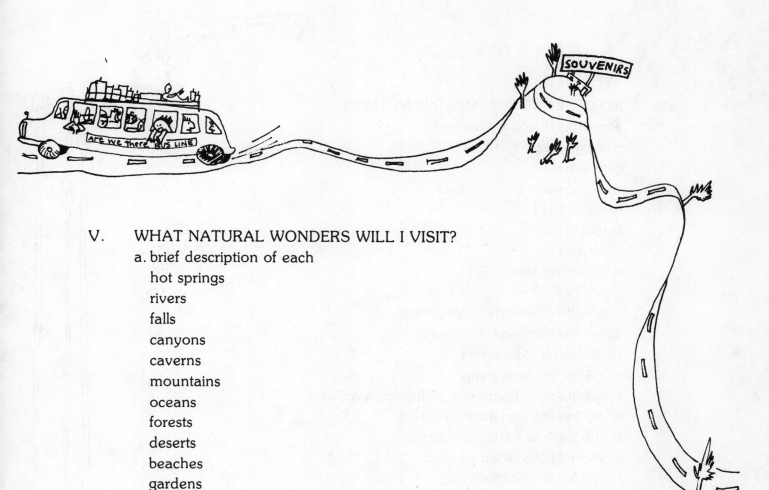

V.   WHAT NATURAL WONDERS WILL I VISIT?
       a. brief description of each
            hot springs
            rivers
            falls
            canyons
            caverns
            mountains
            oceans
            forests
            deserts
            beaches
            gardens
            volcanoes
            farmlands
            bird sanctuaries
            swamps
            mines
            fjords
            cliffs
       b. location of each place

VI.   WHAT CLOTHES WILL I PACK? (list garments)
       a. weight limitations
       b. season of year and temperatures
       c. laundry problems
       d. walking shoes
       e. carry-on luggage
       f. backpack

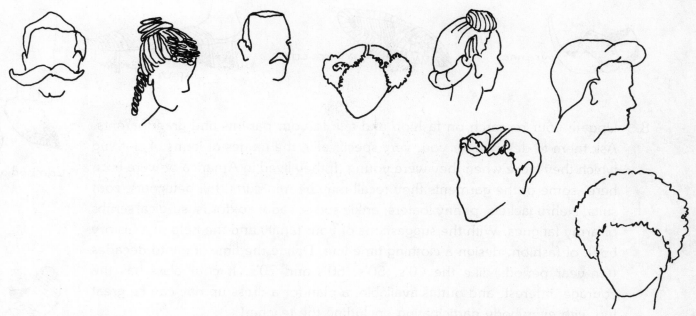

7. We cannot forget our debt to Levi Strauss (1829-1902), the dry goods merchant who was an immigrant to America from Bavaria. He travelled to San Francisco to sell trousers to gold miners and also took with him bolts of canvas which he planned to sell as equipment for the Conestoga covered wagons. When he arrived, a conversation with a prospector revealed that the miners' trousers could not withstand the hard wear of tough work. The pockets would constantly tear when stuffed with gold nuggets. This bit of information gave Mr. Strauss an idea. He took the canvas to a tailor, gave him directions to make trousers and insisted that rivets be used to attach the pockets. And so, out of Strauss' ingenuity, Levis were born! To find out just how popular Levis have become, look through newspapers and magazines to find out how often they are advertised. How many ads can you find? How many different styles of writing do you find in these ads? What are designer jeans, what are their names and why do people buy them instead of cheaper jeans?* Discuss. Cut out this assortment of ads and paste them on construction paper to include in your fashion scrapbook.

---

*A teacher in Warren, Michigan, returned from a trip to Greece and Egypt in 1981 with the observation that the most frequent request she heard was for American jeans, because they were so highly valued.

pyrennes

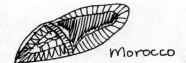
Morocco

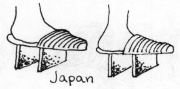
Japan

Cambodia

8. Update your research on fashion and talk to your parents and grandparents. Ask them to describe for you, very specifically, the names of items of clothing which they wore when they were young. If they lived in America or were born here, some of the garments they recall may be miniskirts, full petticoats, zoot suits, Nehru jackets, penny loafers, ankle socks, saddle oxfords, surgical scrubs or army fatigues. With the suggestions of your family and the help of a history book of fashion, design a clothing time line. Divide the time line into decades (ten-year periods) like the 40's, 50's, 60's and 70's. If your class has the courage, interest, and outfits available, a plan for a dress-up day can be great fun with everybody participating--including the teacher!

Argentina

9. Nothing seems funnier to us than fashions of times gone by. A look into an old Sears, Roebuck catalogue will prove this to you! Create your very own HISTORY OF FASHION 19(today's date). Use pictures of men, women and children from the newspapers and magazines. Include formal and informal wear. Don't forget to use fashion magazines, which are often the most outrageous. Cut out the pictures and paste them into a booklet. Record the source, date, and a one-sentence statement below each picture since some outfits have to be explained. You may even want to include the advertising blurb. Put it away carefully for ten years--make a promise to yourself not to throw it out. Take the booklet out again after that time. Show it to family, friends, your children or nieces and nephews. Laugh your heads off!

Greece

Yugoslavia

Tattoo of Berber woman

10. Cosmetics are used to compliment the face, to cover defects, or to emphasize the features. Different paints, dyes, and emollients are used in the preparation of cosmetics. In some cultures, cosmetics are also used by men in varying degrees and for various purposes. The name of Cleopatra comes to mind in the discussion of cosmetics, and rightly so, for two thousand years ago this Egyptian queen was famous for her skill and artistry with makeup. The techniques of the Egyptians were so excellent that archaeologists found still-fragrant cosmetics buried with the mummies in centuries old tombs. Look up the history of cosmetics in the library. Read the reasons for their use in different cultures. Include any fascinating information you find on this topic. Keep notes. With this information, write a cosmetic advertisement for an ancient, modern or futuristic culture. Sell these products successfully. Why do you think there are federal laws which govern the sale of cosmetics in this country?

NAME _____

DATE _____

PURPOSE: To appreciate that people in every culture have a great variety of ways
to beautify and adorn themselves.

1. On the back, list all the persons you interviewed. Also list books, magazines,
pamphlets, family documents, and any other sources used for information.

2. THE MOST EXCITING THINGS I LEARNED: